WHEN

AUTISM

BECOMES THE NEW

AWESOME

*The Story of How My Son Beat the Odds
and Secrets Parents Need to Know*

Transcendent
—Publishing—

TANIA MALANIAK

Transcendent Publishing
PO Box 66202
St. Pete Beach, FL 33736
(800) 232-5087
www.TranscendentPublishing.com

ISBN-13: 978-1-7320764-2-6
Library of Congress: 2018954798

Cover Design by Michelle Gordon

Printed in the United States of America.

This book is dedicated to all parents of autistic children.

We are a strong bunch, and that's why we are the chosen ones. Let's take a life-changing leap forward into a beautiful and fulfilling future with our brilliant kids!

CONTENTS

ACKNOWLEDGMENTS

I'd like to thank all the people who have been a part of our lives – those with the largest rolls, as well as those with the smallest. Every human interaction, both positive and negative, has had an immense influence on our life story - as every interaction has, somehow, shaped the outcome.

To the eye-rollers at the mall (during Cade's tantrums), to the numbers of schools that rejected our child for his behavioral issues – thank you! Though it hurt at the time, your lack of understanding propelled me to find strength I never knew I had. It is you who reminds me that the Universe is always here to serve us all, even when we think the cards are stacked against us.

I'd like to thank all the special individuals who work as ABA / IBI therapists, clinicians, doctors, and Special Education teachers / assistants who bring so much enrichment to the lives of people with autism, and who work so hard finding solutions to bettering these people's lives. For those who have personally impacted our lives – thank you.

This book would never even have been started if it weren't for the "angels" or "energies" that kept me awake one night insisting that I would never sleep again until I agreed to share my story. I know that I was merely a vessel for their message. Thank you for choosing me, and thank you for my countless blessings.

I feel blessed and honored to have had "Sarah" in our lives. She, undeniably, was my greatest teacher of all-things-autism. Her encouragement, advice, passion, knowledge, and all the extra, personal time she spent teaching me everything she knows will be cherished until I die. I love you and thank you, Sarah.

I am so lucky to have come from such loving parents, Cesare and Angela Folco, and loveable, goof-ball, younger brother, Mauro. From the time of diagnosis to today, my family has been some of Cade's most enthusiastic cheerleaders. Thank you for always seeing and acknowledging his strengths and talents, putting him up on pedestals, and bragging shamelessly to strangers about their grandson who beat all odds. I love you.

Thank you to my beautiful in-laws, Michael and Christine Malaniak, and to James' siblings, Michael, Sandee, and Sharon, and their families. Your unconditional love has been felt in so many ways during our journey and it has truly been a source of light in our lives. No distance has ever impeded the flow of love you sent up to us in Canada. The result of that love is immeasurable. I love you.

I cannot express in enough words the love I have for the little people God brought into my life. Cade and Nève are the most miraculous gifts from heaven I could have ever hoped for. They enrich my life on levels I never thought existed. I want to thank them simply for their love, their laughter, and being such great kids.

I saved the MVP for the end - my husband and best friend, James. During this journey of parenthood, I have been through a rollercoaster of emotions. You have seen my ugliest state, and helplessly witnessed me falling into a downward-spiral, but you never gave up on me. Even when I was impossible to live with, your love never left. Thank you for your undying love, patience and prayers, for without which I would not likely be in this peaceful state. You are my rock. You lift me up. You have been nothing short of a miracle in my life. I'm so grateful we chose each other to share in this adventure of life. Thank you, and I love you so much!

INTRODUCTION

My friend, Sarah, and I were sitting in an A&W restaurant for a quick snack. We lived about forty-five minutes away from each other so it seemed like a decent halfway point to meet. I handed Sarah the drawing of a multi-colored train drawn by my son, Cade, who was a student of hers. She always loved Cade's drawings and thought it would be appropriate if he helped with the design of her new business cards and pamphlets. Sarah had previously asked me if Cade would like to draw a train so that she could use it for her cards. I was so moved by the request that I immediately got Cade to draw the picture.

The conversation was focused on my two kids. She loved hearing about Cade's progress, and she was so proud of how far we had all come as a family. She asked about Nève, my daughter, who is two years younger than my boy. Sarah and I had known each other for at least seven years at this point; she came into our lives when Nève was in my womb in the second trimester.

I spent a good portion of our meeting shamelessly purging to her about how wonderfully everything had been going for us. Sarah met me when I was at my lowest state of wellbeing, in a state of deep despair and desperation. I have since come to a much different place in my life – a lighter place.

I explained how Cade's mental development had improved in a most miraculous way, since the first time she started working with him at the age of two. I told her that I had come across some amazing revelations that contributed enormously to Cade's extraordinary transformation. I praised Sarah with great appreciation for her contribution to Cade's unexpected outcome. She had taught me more,

I think, than she could have ever taught my son, though it was he who she was paid to teach. Yes, Sarah did her job skillfully and very effectively as Cade's therapist, but it was her strong words, advice and compassion for our whole family that lit a fire under my feet which ultimately resulted in my son's "perfect" current state.

Sarah said, "Tania, you have to write a book about your experiences. Your knowledge is invaluable to other parents. Your perspective is so raw and natural that I think you could help so many."

I got really excited by the idea. In fact, it wasn't the first time it had been suggested to me. I'd already considered taking on such an endeavor as writing a book to help other parents in similar situations.

After my meeting with Sarah, I put off the idea for a while. After all, it's quite a commitment that requires discipline, free time, and surely some writing talent, which I hoped I had acquired after only receiving a high-school diploma. But, my experiences *are* invaluable, and regardless of how the words are written, the message could be life-changing for many. But, again, I had put the project on hold and I procrastinated because the thought of writing a book was daunting, to say the least, and time was not a luxury. But then one late night, I was struggling to get to sleep (which was a very rare thing) because I could swear I heard voices reprimanding me. They said, "How dare you put this book off!"

"You have been given a gift. You better do this soon."

"Stop procrastinating, Tania!"

"What are you waiting for?"

"Mothers everywhere need you."

This went on for hours during a twilight-like sleep. I just couldn't stop the voices. This had never, ever happened before and I found it a bit disconcerting. My husband was asleep. He's always telling me that there are a lot of "energies" in our bedroom – that's how he describes supernatural entities, but that's a different story for later.

Finally, I lost my patience. I opened my eyes widely and screamed in my head, "OK! I'll start tomorrow! I promise!"

The voices stopped instantly, and I sensed that there was an air of great satisfaction around me. Like angels or other benevolent "energies" were laughing at how they got me to agree to their demands. They must have known I was telling the truth because I never heard from any of them again.

The very next day, I began to write. It took me about two and a half years to complete this book because I could only dedicate one day per week to writing it due to the time constraints associated with working a full-time job, a part-time job, being a mother, and a wife... (and lazy). I knew that if I would be committed to completing this story, it didn't matter to the "energies" how long I'd take.

So, I've welcomed this book-writing endeavor as a mission from God since Him and his night-time, angel-like posse orchestrated me to do this. With all my heart, I hope you enjoy and embrace what I have to share.

CHAPTER 1

THE PURPOSE
OF THIS BOOK
AND THE BEGINNING
OF OUR JOURNEY

The people I have in mind while writing this book are mainly the moms and dads who may have recently received a diagnosis of Autism Spectrum Disorder for their child or children. My purpose for writing this book is to offer help, support, encouragement, advice, love – but mostly – hope, hope and more hope that real and positive change *can* happen.

This *is* a story of hope, inspiration, faith, love, miracles and the human spirit.

There are a million books out there about Defeating Autism Now (DAN) that focus on balancing the biochemistry of the child through diets, herbal remedies and other holistic approaches. I think those books are very important and I encourage you to read at least one, however, I found through my personal experience that no remedy was more effective than the positive energy that the mother carries. I realize that this might sound simplistic and even a bit out-there, but my son's greatest turn-around occurred when I changed my energy patterns, which I will later explain in detail.

I will write about the day to day scenarios that occurred with my son, and the difficult challenges we faced as a family. I am certain that many of these stories will sound eerily familiar to you. I will recount my feelings of devastation and mourning that I know are shared by most in our situation, and how those negative feelings we bear affect our children.

I will discuss hands-on strategies that I have applied with my son that have worked tremendously well, and still continue today. Also, I want to persuade you to change your mind-set about how you address your child and how you confront your child.

I will start from the very beginning of our life-journey from the time of our son's birth; otherwise, there will be less understanding and appreciation for the remarkable ending.

***

James and I were never religious though we were both brought up Catholic. We were the types to never discuss God or religion stuff, but when Cade was born, a spiritual window opened for me. I knew at that moment that something much greater than biology had brought Cade into our lives.

This heartfelt journey begins on the day of my first child's birth on January 22, 2003, in a hospital north of Toronto, Canada. Though my husband, James, and I guessed that we were having a girl, we were overjoyed with surprise to have a beautiful, bouncing baby boy. He was born weighing 8 lbs and 12 oz. Maybe needless to say, my 5'3'' height and small frame wasn't quite structured to handle such a big bundle of love, so he was born by C-section to my disappointment. That disappointment quickly faded when I saw my healthy, fair-skinned, black-haired and blue-eyed little miracle I lovingly called my "Eskimo Baby." He had eyes shaped like almonds and his ebony hair stuck straight up. All bundled-up in his receiving blanket, he looked like a beautiful baby of the North. My husband, James, and

I named him Cade. Since our last name is sort of long and somewhat complicated, we wanted single-syllable names for our children. The name, Cade, is a Welsh name that means "battler" or "warrior." Wow! In hindsight I realize how appropriately we had chosen.

Throughout my youth to present, I have never engaged in the use of recreational drugs or binge drinking. I have always been mindful of my health. During my pregnancy, I started seeing a naturopath – I was really drawn to the world of alternative and natural medicine, and I knew I would raise my kids with a "clean" lifestyle. "Clean" is a term used in the alternative medicine world to describe foods, detergents and body products, such as lotions and hair products that are free from the artificial chemicals that could lead to imbalances in the human body. Pharmaceuticals and medications would be used only as a last resort after trying other natural means to remedy an ailment or sickness. I wanted to follow this healthy-living lifestyle from every moment of my pregnancy to the time my kids would gain their independence. I exercised, ate organic food when possible, had no alcohol, and suffered headaches, colds and even bronchitis without taking any over-the-counter or prescribed medications. I figured I'd give my baby the best start in life that I could possibly offer. I wanted so much to birth Cade the natural way with no epidural, but when his scheduled birth was nearing two weeks overdue and no sign of any action, doctors discovered that the circumference of the baby's head was larger than that of my pelvis. The doctor described it as inserting a square peg into a round hole. This led to a C-section operation being scheduled for a couple of days later.

When the day of the C-section came, everything went as well as one would hope. While I was recovering in the hospital, the nurse came by a few times to check if I had taken my pain killers. She was concerned that I had not taken any pills. I told her that I did not feel comfortable taking a chemical pill since I was breastfeeding. She tried to reassure me that it would not get into the milk. I pride myself on being a pretty logical person – if I ingest something, how do we know what does or doesn't go to the baby's milk? It just didn't sound logical to me. So, I told her I was feeling fine and did not need them, which was the truth. Then I explained that I had been taking a homeopathic remedy called Arnica, which aids with healing, bruising and pain. I healed gorgeously and every time I sensed pain coming on, I would take the Arnica. In mere minutes, the pain would drastically subside. She said, "Would you write that down for me please? I think other patients would like this."

Since then, James and I have become more enthusiastic about "clean" living. I've also gained a ton of knowledge on homeopathic medicine because I've had such great success with it. We even decided to vaccinate Cade homeopathically. Homeopathic medicine is a natural practice that treats and strengthens one's constitution through the harnessed energies of minerals, plants and animals. Yeah... look it up. There was a lot of controversy over the safety of mainstream vaccines at the time, so I approached this decision with some firm opposition from my pediatrician, but lots of support from James and my parents. I followed my gut. I always think that's the right thing to do.

Being that Cade was the very first baby to be born in my family among my cousins and brother, I had no idea what was to be expected. When we brought Cade home, he slept a lot! It was to my understanding that that was normal for a newborn. He also ate a lot! When he would arise from his slumbers, he'd eat fiercely as I nursed him. I've heard that some babies could take up to an hour to feed, but not Cade. He'd suck it down in ten minutes max. Sometimes, he'd feed too quickly that it would explode out of him immediately afterwards and we'd have to start all over again. Looking back, it sounds hilarious, but I can assure you it was not funny at the time. I was very conscientious about everything I consumed since I worried so much about him. Still no wine... boy, did I want it!

Cade became stronger and chunkier throughout the weeks, gaining weight well. But things were becoming more difficult – the already tiresome nights became even harder for us. Cade would wake-up throughout the night screaming bloody murder. I would feed him and that would calm him briefly, but after he unlatched he'd go back to screaming inconsolably. Was it gas? I didn't know. There's only so many ways you can try to burp your baby before you suspect there might be something else disturbing him. I would change a mildly dampened diaper in hope that that was the cause for all the ado. Still, nothing seemed to settle the screams of this poor kid. One night, out of exhausted frustration, I cradled him securely in my arms and I began to bounce. I discovered that the higher I leaped, pranced and bounded across the nursery floor, the calmer Cade became. Eventually, he'd fall asleep. Would you believe it if I told you that I would have to do this for two hours straight, twice a night for about six months? Well, I did. One would think that I'd lose a ton of baby fat doing this midnight marathon, but no such luck. Where was James? He was in bed awake, trying to rest-up for work the next morning. I know he was tortured over both Cade's and my long, difficult nights. From the beginning, I offered to be the parent who'd get up during the night, since I had the likely opportunity to nap in the day while being at home raising Cade. While I'd be leaping around, singing lullabies, James would often check-up on us. Sometimes, Cade would be just about unconscious, and James would whisper something to me through the crack of the door like, "Are you OK?" This would alert Cade and get him screaming again! And then I would start screaming at James, "Get out! Get out!" James would sneak back to bed remorsefully and with concern for me and my laborious task ahead.

We continued seeing the naturopath in the hope of getting some help for our colicky little one. I wondered how much it helped, if at all. Even if it was helping to some degree, I couldn't imagine it being worse than this! Cade's pediatrician didn't have much advice that was helpful and there wasn't anything medically he could do. When Cade would finally fall asleep he slept well, but he would just scream his brains out when he was awake, even during the day. It only got worse as he got older. Naturally, by the third month the naps became shorter and the awake-time became longer. I was beginning to lose my mind and my tolerance was growing very thin. My gentle consoling rarely worked. Cade would stop crying by being tossed or played with vigorously. He liked large movements like heavy swinging. I noticed that Cade reacted well to my singing too. James and I got Cade an electric swinger, and a Jolly Jumper, which allows a small baby to jump. I found it strange and amusing, however, that Cade loved to spin while in his Jolly Jumper. Sometimes he would spend the entire time spinning clockwise then counter-clockwise, like a figure skater. His eyes would be fixated to the floor beneath his feet. Just when I'd think he'd get so dizzy he'd puke, he'd just spin the other way. I thought, *can't wait to get this kid on a roller coaster!* These toys were a great investment because they brought Cade and me a lot of peace.

Cade was about 5 months old when the sunny days of spring and then summer rolled around. I found that long brisk walks in the stroller were very soothing to both of us. We would leave the house with our dog, Charlie, and not return for hours. I loved those walks. I would sing songs the entire way so that he would know that I was always there. I learned that Cade constantly needed movement. When he would cry uncontrollably, the bigger the movement, the happier (or quieter) he became. I had become a very tired, tired mommy.

I remember one outing when I took Cade and my mom to a friend's restaurant in Toronto. I was so excited to get out of the house and have a nice lunch out with my mom and introduce Cade to some of the staff members who had watched my tummy get bigger throughout my pregnancy. My mother and I sat down, upon a high chair by our side perched the car-seat in which Cade sat, we ordered our food, and then began to relax and enjoy our drinks. A few minutes later, something set off Cade. He began fussing gradually getting louder, so I took him out of his car-seat and checked for obvious things like whether he had a full diaper, if he was hungry or had gas. After I realized that none of those issues were the cause of his malcontent, his fussing began to escalate further. My mom then took him into her arms and tried to calm him. By then, Cade had begun screaming constantly and loudly to the point where restaurant patrons and servers were all looking over. My mom took him outside thinking that the fresh air and city activity would settle him. Cade continued screaming unfazed by the distractions. I sat at the table watching my mother and the baby through the window, still able to hear the screams. I was getting anxious as I sensed my mom was feeling helpless, so I went outside to try to help her. I took Cade and began bouncing him around. That heavy bouncing sort of began to calm him but I didn't have two hours to do this outside the restaurant. I urged my mom to go back to the table as our pizzas had arrived. From the window, I gestured for her to start eating and that I'd be in shortly. I knew that that wasn't really going to be the case. I knew this was the end of my lunch date with Mom. I must have been out there for twenty minutes before my mother, feeling dreadful, came out and said, "Let's take shifts. Your pizza's getting cold."

I responded, "Would you mind if we took everything to go?" And so that was the end of that. Cade hollered most of the way home.

> *From about three weeks old, I found out that Cade needed **big** movements to get any relief. This continued for months.*

CHAPTER 2

NO PROGRESS,
NO AWARENESS...
IS CADE DEAF?

By the time Cade was a year old, he had started to grow out of the lengthy, colic-like crying episodes, but that didn't mean that it was all roses from here on. In fact, things were more difficult at times. He had not spoken or walked at all yet, and the idea of him walking still seemed several months away since he even struggled with crawling. Instead of getting on all fours, my little "warrior" would do what appeared to be a military style belly wriggle, his forearms leading the way. I expressed my concerns to his pediatrician, but Dr. Hanley reassured me that boys sometimes take a little longer to develop these skills. He comforted me, "I didn't walk until I was eighteen months... and here I am."

I remember still feeling disappointed with his delayed progress. Most of the other babies at the play groups were walking and some had communication abilities. This frustrated me because I thought Cade was just a really laid-back kid who wasn't easily motivated. I wanted him to get going! I wanted him to say something, anything! I wanted to see him interact with the other toddlers instead of avoiding them. I wanted to see him play with toys like the others. Instead, Cade would take the smaller parts of toys, wave them in front of his eyes, and then chuck them across the room repeatedly and obsessively. It looked disturbing to me. We'd often let Cade play in the gated den near the kitchen where we kept all the toys in a chest. When I'd check on him minutes later, it always seemed as though there'd been an explosion of Lego and blocks. Cade would compulsively and repeatedly wave an item on the left side of his eyes in sort of a demonic way, and then launch it over his left shoulder. Cade would also take toy cars and trucks, turn them upside-down, and spin the wheels for a totally inappropriate length of time while staring at the spinning wheel. He had no interest in playing with toys the way they were intended. Furthermore, he never looked at me.

You know, it's strange – up until this time, Cade hadn't given any indication that he had much awareness of James or me. It was sort of like he knew we were around but was indifferent to us. James and I had been out of town for five days and my parents had been looking after Cade at their place. We were so excited to see our little man that we could hardly contain ourselves. When we entered the room, Cade looked up at us in his high chair and began to wail. James and I were taken aback. We'd hoped that we would be greeted with a smile at best, but this reaction to our return was startling. We approached Cade for some hugs and kisses. Instead, Cade pushed us away. My parents found his reaction so funny, they laughed loudly. I was hurt. Cade seemed angry with us. My father remarked, "Cade must be angry you left him. Look how smart he is to be reacting to you this way." It was as if Cade was communicating, "How dare you leave me for so long! I'm so mad at you, Mommy and Daddy!"

Well, it wasn't the reaction we expected or hoped for, but it was demonstrative that Cade had the capacity to express himself, and to have awareness. He had never shown any of these attributes before. After we got over our hurt feelings from Cade's rejection, we realized that there was potential there for us to break through his tough shell. He knew we were his parents, and he had affection for us.

I enrolled Cade into the local Gymboree. It's a cute program for babies and toddlers, and their parents or guardians to playfully interact with one another through imagination, music and movement. I figured that if he spent more time with other toddlers, he'd learn by their example. Things seemed fine during the first visit, but each week after became increasingly more difficult. During circle-time, Cade would become distracted by the colorful playground at the other side of the room. Uninterested in the music lesson going on, he would squirm out of my arms trying to get to the slides and obstacle course. The more I tried redirecting him to the lesson at hand, the more he fought against me until a full-on meltdown would occur. I knew his tantrums were out of the norm because of the awestruck looks the other parents gave us. Even the tiny tots stopped what they were doing in amazement of witnessing Cade's wrath. Cade's behavior paralyzed the room. I was stubborn, I would not give in to his desire to leave the circle because I knew his indifference to the circle activities was abnormal, and by God my kid was NOT going to be the abnormal one! Besides, I'm not the type of parent who allows their kid to do whatever he wants at any time he wants just because he's little. I wanted my kid to understand that rules are made to be followed like in the real world, and the sooner the child learns this, the better. But, after disrupting the group with Cade's unrelenting screams for such a prolonged period, and after I couldn't ignore the understandable dirty looks from the other parents and instructor anymore, I would take him out into the hallway while I attempted to settle him down unsuccessfully. This happened every week thereafter – to the *disappointment* of the other families – until I finally quit the program.

A small weight had been lifted from my shoulders when Cade finally took his first steps at eighteen months, just like Dr. Hanley had suggested, but he still wasn't communicating. Now that Cade was walking, the destruction of our playroom had become much greater. It was harder to keep him safe and confined from dangerous situations, but I'm sure that's something all parents experience when their babies turn into toddlers. With the newly acquired skill of walking came new and unusual behaviors and more cause for concern. When Cade would roam around the kitchen, he'd go to the corner and walk from one wall to the other, back and forth. It appeared weird, but I was still not prepared to address that he had a problem. My mom chalked everything up to Cade being a late bloomer who needed extra time to mature. I wanted so much to believe that.

My parents-in-law lived in New Jersey at the time. They were showered with new grand-babies all at once. A new grand-baby was born every year and Cade was grandson number three. My parents-in-law had a good amount of experience being parents of four children, and grandparents to three thus far. Eventually, that number would grow to seven. On their second visit to us since Cade's birth, my father-in-law, Mike, pulled James aside and expressed his concern over Cade's mannerisms. He played differently from his other two grandsons, Matthew and Cooper. With sensitivity, he suggested to James that he may need to be assessed by a doctor.

James and I quietly knew that something seemed strange, but not a word about it was uttered until he told me what his dad said. Our natural response was denial, of course. Yet, the responsible thing to do was to bring up these concerns at Cade's next pediatric appointment. Dr. Hanley had finally retired at the age of eighty, so we brought Cade to see our family practitioner, Dr. Wertman. She said that he was much too young to come to any conclusions since Cade wasn't two yet, but it would be wise to keep our attention on his progress, or lack thereof.

Except for a few words like "Mama" and "Dada," Cade didn't say much at all. I was not only frustrated and annoyed by this, I was really worried. The other toddlers I saw were much more communicative and had a much more elaborate vocabulary. Cade seemed oblivious to the world around him and to my verbal interactions.

Most of the time, Cade appeared only to engage with me when I sang to him. When he wanted or needed something, I wouldn't know it because he would just have a meltdown, seemingly over everything and nothing in particular. Quickly approaching the age of two, Cade still could not form a three-word sentence or grasp the idea that a single spoken word could communicate a need. For Cade, words were only used to label items. He gave me no indication of what was going on in his mind. Most non-verbal toddlers would point at a desired item and maybe grunt or fuss. Cade did not know *how* to point. He had absolutely no natural ability to communicate.

I enrolled him in a sign language for toddlers group for a short time. The people who run this program believe that this helps babies and toddlers to communicate with more ease and helps them foster verbal communication. Cade was present in body, but he wasn't present in mind during these circle groups. I placed my hands over his, and we did the motions for 'I want', 'more', 'milk', 'cookie', and every animal under the sun, every week for two months. I tried using this method at home, but Cade struggled to even look at me, let alone look at me signing and hence teaching *him* to sign. Later, I realized that this method was like teaching your child to depend on a crutch unnecessarily. If your child is capable of making sounds and/or words with their mouth, then words through speech should be the only form of communication one should teach, in my opinion.

My mother-in-law often reminded me that my husband didn't talk until he was three. A couple of others also told me that their sons didn't say a word until that age. One stranger I met at a bagel shop was nice enough to share that her son didn't speak until he was three and now he was a successful lawyer. I grasped and held on to those little anecdotal nuggets because they truly brought me the hope I so profoundly craved. So, I felt it was reasonable for us to set the goal that Cade would be speaking by the time he turned three.

Sometimes I'd wake up in the morning and find it excruciating to face the day, but I refused to let the chips fall the way they were falling. My ego and fear drove me to continue working with Cade every chance I had. I'd engage him with my songs and long stroller walks which would be interrupted with hours of playtime at the local playground. I would take him out to a few different Mom and Tot play-groups as much as possible. I took him all over the city trying to expose him to all sorts of wonders, with the hope that we'd find something that would excite and awaken him. One beautiful spring day, I decided to take Cade to Harbour Front, a lovely marina in Toronto, part of Lake Ontario, where you could find shops, restaurants, and buskers. It seemed that there was a different festival going on every weekend. I would point things out to Cade like, "See the big boat, Cade?" and follow that up with a song from the Wiggles, "The friendly pirate ship is rocking on the sea..." Unless I sang, I don't think Cade would've connected with me, for music was all he seemed to be able to hear at the time. For a second, Cade would reward me with a grin, though I don't think he processed the link between the ship at the dock and the Wiggles' song.

Further along the boardwalk we would pass the docked sailboats and sometimes we'd see happy boat owners just thrilled about the upcoming summer weather. Further still, we'd come across a flock of birds in a quiet area with little human interference. I remember stopping there with Cade as he was sitting contently in his stroller. Some of the birds were flying close to us while others floated peacefully on the lake's surface. There were mallard ducks, seagulls and swans. I got down on my knees beside Cade expecting to see him react to all the busy fowl. To my disappointment, his eyes were lifeless, as if these birds and I weren't even there. I wasn't going to accept that. Again, I began singing to Cade loudly, all the passers-by could hear, and I didn't care. I sang the duck songs, Old McDonald, and anything that referenced birds while clapping my hands and pointing at them. I made loud quacking, honking, chirping and cooing sounds as I sang loudly. Trust me when I say I was making a complete ass of myself! But it didn't matter for a second because I began to see a tiny spark in Cade's eyes. I saw a moment of AWARENESS. That tiny spark was definitely worth the asinine public performance. Though it was just for a minute, it was real and very meaningful. I realized that Cade had the potential to do that again and maybe for a longer period.

Not a day went by where I wouldn't sing all kinds of children's songs to Cade, even the couple of Italian and French ones I learned from my grandparents and grade-school teachers. At this point in Cade's life, I had acquired a massive repertoire of songs in my brain, which I learned from the giant library of kiddy DVDs and CDs we'd collected and enjoyed over several months. When I got sick of hearing myself sing the same tunes repeatedly, I started making up my own. I figured out that this was a somewhat effective way of getting Cade to hear me say that I love him. And maybe this was the key to getting him to talk and be like the other kids.

Another way of trying to engage with Cade was to take him to the swings at the park. Cade loved the swings as early as 4 or 5 months. I would push him high – higher than a baby his age would normally be pushed. Cade was a physically strong baby with excellent control of his head and body. I'd sing to him, of course, as I pushed him. I knew he was having the time of his life because he was peaceful and content. After spending a minimum of an hour on the swings, I would take Cade to the slide or the climbing bars. He didn't care for those things at all, but I'd take him anyway with the desire of broadening his interests. One day at the playground, when Cade was about twenty months, an event took place that would change my life forever.

We had just finished playing on the swings and I had placed Cade on the ground to walk to the next activity, when all of a sudden, he began to sprint. I called out to him to stop but he continued. So, I ran after him, calling, "Cade! Stop!" But he just wouldn't stop, and I remember being surprised by how fast his little legs took him. I was right behind him, yet I just couldn't nab him. "Cade! Cade!" I yelled frantically as he would soon begin approaching the street. I bolted toward him and grabbed his shoulders as I fell to my knees. I was so angry that I yelled at the top of my lungs, "Cade!" one last time right to the back of his head. Cade didn't react. Not so much as a flinch. Was Cade deaf, or partially deaf?

I couldn't explain why he responded to my singing but not to my panicked command. Even my dog, Charlie, responded to my panicked voice when I commanded him. When the second hearing test showed no problems with Cade's hearing, my suspicions were confirmed that we were dealing with something more serious. I felt sick to my stomach. My dreams of having a brilliant and healthy child were no longer realistic to me. Even with all the hints that led up to this moment, this was truly the first time I knew Cade was handicapped. I never told a soul.

The next few months became harder for my family, but mostly for me since I was home alone with Cade. His behavior got more uncontrollable and unpredictable. I would dread going to the grocery store or mall. I remember Cade screaming violently while sitting in the shopping cart at the grocery store on many occasions. I don't mean the kind of tantrums that most parents experience when their child doesn't get what they want, I mean, Cade would have such a meltdown he would attempt to throw himself off the cart while biting, kicking and punching me. This would go on for about two hours. It almost seemed like he had been possessed by demons. The most benign thing to a regular kid would set off Cade. For instance, with Cade in the shopping cart, I'd be going up and down the aisles of the produce section and I'd realize that I'd forgotten to grab something I had already passed, so I would have to backtrack a few steps. This would ignite a firestorm within Cade and I would be kicking myself for the next two hours or so while struggling to control his violence. I would have to hold him down using all my strength, preventing him from hurting us both. I think the worst part of this, besides the obvious, was the wonderful looks of judgement I got from people, shaking their heads in disapproval and uttering words under their breath. I can't really blame these folks – I was one of them before Cade came into my life. I often thought parents of screaming children should discipline them firmly and take them out of the store or place of business. I still believe that. In my situation, however, Cade could not be moved easily. He could not hear me or see me while he punched the air, whacking his head and biting on the hand bar of the cart in his fit of rage. He did not respond to my raised voice, or my hands-on firm manipulations. Some trips to the market would end with us exiting the store leaving a cart filled with groceries abandoned in an aisle.

During Cade's toddlerhood, I don't recall ever having to wear an actual coat in the dead of a Canadian winter because sweating profusely through my clothes was a daily occurrence. The psychological strain of knowing what the day would entail, alone, was enough to turn me into a walking furnace. Not to mention that I was physically pushed to the max regularly throughout the day. Come to think of it, I don't remember an instance when I didn't sport that ever so sexy soaked armpit look during that time in Cade's life.

I had this delusional idea that I may have had the power to produce an intelligent and healthy child because I did all the right things during my pregnancy. I ate organically, I avoided medication, I would put headphones to my belly every night, so the baby could listen to Mozart to enhance and nurture brain development. I even didn't allow Cade to have any vaccinations (contrary to the advice of Dr. Hanley) because the controversies surrounding the safety of childhood vaccines were at their peak. I went the homeopathic route for inoculations instead.

I see now how remarkably arrogant, naive and foolish I was to believe I had *any* power over the outcome of my child's developmental and physical health. The destructive mindset I placed upon myself, the control I thought I had, and these high standards and expectations that I had set for my child unknowingly lit the fuel to spiraling into a dark state of mind that would lead me to depression, resentment and shame.

As Cade moved from a baby to a toddler he demonstrated little to no awareness. Yet, tiny sparks of awareness would peek through when I sang animatedly, danced vigorously, and clapped loudly. Try to recognize when those sparks of awareness happen with your child and do more of that to keep them outside their "cocoon."

They told me not to worry, but you can't ignore a mother's intuition – it's unlike any other force. Listen to it and trust it!

CHAPTER 3

THE DIAGNOSIS

One of my all-time favorite movies is Rain Man starring Dustin Hoffman and Tom Cruise. It's a film about an autistic man who was institutionalized in an era when Autism Spectrum Disorder (ASD) was a condition not yet widely understood, or even recognized as a disorder of neurodevelopment. I watched that movie so much as a teen because the characters and storyline moved me deeply. I was fascinated by the symptoms of an autistic person, which were so accurately represented by Dustin Hoffman. The way his character, Raymond Babbitt, reacted during situations that forced him to veer away from his regular schedule would cause him to enter such a frenzy whereby he'd hit himself in the head and yell a series of words over and over again. I was living in a reality-version of this movie that starred Cade, but I knew I wasn't going to allow his future to turnout like that of Raymond. Not over my dead body.

I kept my opinions and observations to myself, however. The idea of having an autistic child was unbearable to me. In fact, I tried to keep the idea hidden away and didn't allow myself to consciously consider the prospect. This is how I tried to deal with the pain. But it was hard to ignore all the weird behavior and lack of developmental progress. I wouldn't dare address any concerns to my family, not even to James. The last thing I wanted to do was to get anyone worried, but I needed to know that he was, indeed, fine, and *not* "Rain Man." I desperately longed for a professional to tell me I was wrong and that I was imagining things. I prayed for someone to tell me he would be perfectly fine and outgrow these behaviors. I needed to hear a specialist say the magic words, "You have nothing to worry about."

I called my sister-in-law, Tatiana, who, now a doctor, had a strong medical background as her dad is a reputable ENT specialist and a surgeon. Tatiana was in medical school at the time and I knew she'd be able to connect me with some child psychologists who ran private practices. I told her that I was concerned about Cade's lack of progress and just wanted to learn strategies to help him along. I later called my mom to let her know my intentions. I didn't tell her the truth... I simply couldn't because I didn't want to face the possibility of having to comfort my mother who might take the news badly. I had enough of my own pain to manage. Tatiana provided me the details of two psychologists. Supposedly, they were the best in their field in Toronto. Cade could not afford to wait around for an appointment with a child psychologist through the public system. I was told that the waiting list could be up to a year, maybe two. So, James and I personally hired one of them to assess Cade immediately.

Dr. Maria Konstance came to our home and watched Cade play. She asked me a million questions about his behavior and mannerisms that I answered candidly and honestly. She performed a few tests on Cade that involved playing games. Some were disheartening to watch. I remember her observing the way Cade played after she had given him some blocks. I warned her that he was just going to launch them one by one across the room, and he did. Dr. Konstance gathered all the blocks and tried again. Cade didn't launch them this time. He lay on his tummy and began to horizontally line the blocks in a single row. Dr. Konstance moved the blocks out from the row and this set Cade off into a full-on meltdown. She ignored his protests and began stacking the blocks on top of each other. "This is how a child would typically play with these blocks," she explained. "Lining them in a row is atypical behavior." After some mild persuasion she got him to do the same. This did not please him at all.

After a two-hour assessment, she gave me her professional opinion. "Well, this is hard because he is not quite two years old and some of these symptoms might correct themselves," I breathed a huge sigh of relief until she continued, "however, I do believe Cade has a degree of autism, but I do not know to what degree at this stage. You have an advantage because you have called me while Cade is still in his early development." She continued, "You and your husband need to work very hard with Cade from here on. I can see he has a chance at a somewhat normal life, but it won't come without extensive therapy and a lot of work on your part." I had that feeling in my stomach like one gets with stage-fright. Out of shear panic I began to bombard her with rhetoric. "How could this happen? I did *everything* right!" "This is not supposed to happen to me and my child!"

Dr. Konstance explained to me something about chromosomes and the Y gene being fragile because it's incomplete hence why so many boys compared to girls are affected by autism... or something. I didn't care. I did *everything* right and this was not supposed to happen. I'd ask, "Do you think he's got a long way to go or not such a long way?" and "Do you think Cade will be verbal soon?" and "What age do you think he'll outgrow this?" and "He WILL outgrow this, right?"

Looking back, I realize how ridiculous these questions were. I must have hoped that "psychologist meant "psychic." As a mother herself, Dr. Konstance was very empathetic and tried comforting me by saying that he was still too young for anyone to know for definite what his future will hold, but with professional help, we'd get positive results. Dr. Konstance was kind, brilliantly intelligent and very professional but I hated the results of her assessment. I simply was not prepared to accept this. I didn't hire her to tell me my son was autistic – I wanted her to tell me everything would be ok! So, I made an appointment with Dr. A. Fabian, the second name on my list. If memory serves me well, he came a day later, and I hoped he was going to provide the good news I was seeking. *"Mrs. Malaniak, Cade is just fine."*

Dr. A. Fabian came to our house. He had a distinct accent, likely Romanian, and he smelled of expensive cologne. I informed him during our first phone call that he was the second child psychologist I'd contacted. I explained that Dr. Konstance had already done an informal assessment on Cade, and that she suspected autism. I told him that I believed she was wrong and Cade needed re-evaluation. He told me that he'd provide a detailed write-up of his observations and we'd take it from there.

Similarly to Dr. Konstance, Dr. Fabian played with Cade for two hours or so. He performed some similar tests and some different ones. While he was analyzing Cade, he also interrupted his inappropriate play with corrections. He offered me valuable tools to help encourage speech. Cade completed one of the tests successfully – using a toddler's toy that involved a ball being hit with a plastic hammer, knocking the ball through a hole so that it would roll down a little maze until it popped back out from the bottom. I was very proud that he did what was expected so I praised Cade with, "Good boy!"

Dr. Fabian suggested that I say, "Good hitting the ball with the hammer, Cade!" instead. Children with communication and speech delays find specific praise far more helpful than a general statement – it helps them to understand what they did specifically to earn the praise. Dr. Fabian offered many different strategies like that to me and he didn't really bring up the topic of autism. I found his recommendations quite helpful; in fact, I still use them today with every little kid I interact with. He also suggested very strongly that I get one of his recommended therapists to come over to the house and begin working with Cade. I thought he was trying to sell me something and I sort of tuned out. He pushed the issue by handing me business cards and calling up the therapist on his cell phone to see if she had availability to take on a new client. I wasn't interested but I pretended I was.

We were asked to go to Dr. Fabian's office for more testing days later. He asked Cade to follow instructions while engaging in more difficult games, activities and tasks. Cade was not very responsive or reactive to Dr. Fabian's verbal cues and requests. It was so discouraging watching Cade failing at everything that was asked of him. Cade was asked to hold a crayon and draw a simple line from dot to dot – it was as if Dr. Fabian was talking to Cade in another language. After a painful hour or so, Dr. Fabian completed his thorough assessment of Cade and he scheduled me to come back to his office a week later to discuss his findings.

A week later I was sitting in Dr. Fabian's waiting room and I remember feeling that stage fright sensation in my gut. Dr. Fabian called me into his office. He gestured for me to sit on the sofa by his desk. Dr. Fabian sat down and began to tell me all about how he thought Cade was adorable and great. While consulting a report printed on blue paper, Dr. Fabian explained all the good aspects of Cade's abilities. This was just to sugar-coat what was to come. He started to discuss in detail all of Cade's delays, inabilities and developmental shortcomings. He compared Cade to a chart of national averages for his age group for cognitive ability, gross and fine motor skills, language, etc. Cade fell behind on every category except fine motor. Some were significantly worse than others. Almost at the age of two, Cade ranked about a full year behind in total. Just so there were no minced words on Dr. Fabian's part, he pulled out another chart, something that I will never in my life forget – it was the Autism Spectrum Disorder chart. He got up from his desk and stood in front of me unfolding this long and narrow scale-chart that spread horizontally. He said while pointing to the left of the paper, "This is the low functioning area of the autistic spectrum where the individual has severe difficulties doing the simple things we do every day, and communication is very limited – in most cases, they are non-verbal." Then he ran his fingers along the width of the chart to the right. "And this is the high-functioning end of the autistic spectrum that is known as Asperger's Syndrome. These individuals are often very intelligent and can do very well in life - this is why it is called Autism Spectrum. There are many degrees of this disorder."

...Why, Cade must be at least in the middle! I thought. Before I could digest all the information, with his hand sliding back to the left of the spectrum Dr. Fabian concluded, "Cade is down here."

I don't recall what occurred immediately after that or what I said. I do remember feeling sick like I had just been kicked in the gut.

As I was leaving the clinic, Dr. Fabian handed me that thick blue report outlining his assessment of Cade. He said, "Keep this report in a safe place. You will need it to help you get services and funding from the government. Also, when you decide to get Cade the proper intervention, the therapist will need this." *Slow down, slow down... what?*

Dr. Fabian had already booked an appointment for a therapist to come to our house. A couple of days later, he and a young woman came to our home. She introduced herself as Lila. Lila seemed very friendly and full of energy. She and Dr. Fabian discussed Cade and his required therapies. They talked to each other while observing and playing with Cade, and Lila wrote copious notes in a binder. Every so often they would include me in the conversation, but it wasn't about me. After a lengthy period of time, Dr. Fabian asked me if I would commit to having a therapist for at least twenty hours a week. I was floored! *Did he say twenty hours a week?* I had a feeling that was going to be mighty expensive – and what a huge invasion of privacy it would be to have someone in our house for that amount of time!

"Really?" I asked, hoping he was actually kidding, "Twenty

hours seems like a lot!"

"It's very necessary," he replied, "I'm not doing this to make money off you. Cade needs help and the more intervention he gets the better chance we will have to correct his behaviors. It's that simple."

That simple, huh?

"Well I can't afford twenty hours a week." I blurted out in aggravation, "Can we start with, maybe, eight hours a week?" I was convinced that was all Cade needed, even *that* was a lot to me.

"It's up to you," Dr. Fabian remarked regretfully. Then he added, "With your permission, we would like to put Cade on the waiting list for government assistance."

I'm not the type of person who ever looks to benefit from anything government-funded or to receive anything I didn't earn directly. I gripe more than I'd like to admit about how the Canadian and Provincial leaders demand way too much from the taxpayers due to the ever-growing "entitlement programs." I simply don't believe in redistribution of wealth.

The idea put a foul taste in my mouth to even consider adding our name to any such list, but I begrudgingly agreed to do just that. I tried justifying it by convincing myself that I deserved some money in return after shelling out – what I feel to be – obscene amounts of our earnings over all these years to the taxman. It still tasted really bad to me though.

"Well, let's start with the eight hours per week and see where it goes," I said.

Cade would begin treatment the following week. And Sarah came into our lives.

If you suspect any kind of delay with your child, react immediately by seeking intervention and advice. Many parents become too terrified to admit or address that their child might have autism that they fall into a state of deep denial and emotional paralyzation. Parents often ignore the facts and put intervention aside for years, hoping that time or ignoring the signs might make it all go away. Inaction on the parents' part is extraordinarily dangerous because intervention is most effective and successful at the very earliest part of a child's life. I was sort of in denial about Cade's diagnosis. I was incapable of admitting that the doctors were right about him being autistic, yet, I knew that he needed treatment to move forward. So, we looked at it as if Cade was being tutored like any other child who was lagging behind in a subject or grade. We knew therapy would provide the swift kick in the ass he needed to catch up.

Put the needs of your child before your ego.

CHAPTER 4

THE INTRODUCTION TO THERAPY

Cade was about nineteen months of age when James and I were elated to learn we would be expecting a second baby. We didn't know yet that she was a girl because we wanted to be surprised again. She would be named Nève, pronounced like Neve Campbell. The spelling means snow in Italian. Poetic, no? If pronounced in Gaelic, it means promising princess.

I treated this pregnancy like the first one. I took extra good care of what I ate and what I did to ensure that I gave this baby every possible health advantage. I was so tormented over the situation with Cade that I didn't focus much of my attention on the baby growing inside me. By that I mean I didn't allow myself to sit back and enjoy experiencing this beautiful miracle occurring within.

All my energy, focus and worries were on Cade.

The idea that the second baby would be at risk of being autistic was the farthest thought from my mind because something profound within me told me that this baby was going to be fine. This may sound odd, but there was a little voice in my head that reassured me. Maybe it was something as primitive as a mother's intuition. Whoever or whatever that voice was, I believed it, and I surrendered to its warm message. I must admit, though, that my lack of worry about Baby Number Two was a little confusing to my usual worry-wart self. Without knowing it, I think this was the first time in my life that I ever truly surrendered my trust to God.

It was the fall of 2004, shortly before we visited with Dr. Konstance and Dr. Fabian. We'd enrolled Cade into the Central Montessori School half-day program where I felt he could develop more speech, gain more independence, and acquire necessary social and academic skills.

I gave the school director the truthful details of Cade's difficulties and challenges, and she reassured me that many kids start off with similar challenges. She suggested that he participate in class for a two-week trial to see how it would go. I felt comfortable with that plan and I was anxious and excited to get him into the program. At this point I knew I couldn't give Cade the learning tools he needed. I remember how adorable he looked as he walked down the hallway of his first school, wearing his blue jeans, GAP knit sweater, and his toddler-sized Dr. Seuss backpack. Sporting a new short haircut, and standing at two feet tall, I was proud that Cade was my tiny little man. He seemed at ease as he approached the classroom. A lovely, young lady (actually, a nineteen-year-old girl) named Sandra met us at the door. She was really pretty, friendly and had a warm smile. I immediately felt calmer after meeting her and the other two wonderful teachers in the class. I reiterated my concerns to them, which included warnings of Cade's potentially damaging fury. They laughed that such a wee, sweet little boy could really be that reckless. They would soon understand as every day I'd receive more stories of hitting, screaming and lack of focus. I would spy on Cade for a few moments in the playground before I was expected for pick-up. He'd be wailing and completely immoveable in Sandra's arms while the other kids played nicely together. There was an endearing playground instance when Cade was being pushed along in a stroller by several little girls while he sobbed inconsolably. One day I was asked to come in a bit earlier before dismissal to talk with one of the head teachers whose name was Farzaneh. She was a really kind-natured, very caring and gentle woman. Cade was sobbing in her arms. "We were in the gym today because of the rain," she began to explain in her Farsi accent, "and all the children screaming hurt Cade's ears. He has been crying so much and covering his ears with his hands, so I brought him back to the classroom. He's just now beginning to calm down." I already knew that Cade's senses were hyper-sensitive, particularly to sounds and bright light, and probably the children's vibrating shrills bouncing off the gymnasium walls was just too agonizing for Cade to bear.

A couple of months later, I regretted hearing that Farzaneh had been moved to a different class and was replaced by a lady whose name I cannot for the life of me remember. I recall not liking her much. She was sort of a know-it-all, impatient type. After a few short days of being Cade's teacher, she approached me, "I believe your son has some form of autism and you need to get him checked by the doctor. He doesn't look in your eyes when you talk to him and he doesn't follow directions. He makes a mess of the toys because he throws them everywhere. Cade plays by himself and doesn't interact with the other students."

I replied with quiet disdain, "I've already had him assessed this week." But all I was thinking was – *What a bitch! Hasn't she ever heard of "compassion," for goodness sake!* Such a difficult and painful subject should be addressed more delicately than that.

Shortly thereafter, Sandra left Central Montessori to further her studies in childhood education. After she left there was no point in Cade staying.

***

We met Sarah, the therapist, for the first time when she arrived at our house on a cool November day. She came to work with Cade eight hours a week for the next few months. She was a very petite, young-looking woman who seemed to stand at no more than four feet and ten inches tall. I remember noticing her big brown eyes surrounded by a radiant, glowing face of flawless bronzed skin. Really, she looked like a walking makeup billboard – absolutely flawless. Sarah was very well put together and every little accessory she wore was just right. Though quite tiny, her personality packed a punch as she exploded with high, but focused, energy.

I took her to meet Cade, who was in the playroom in the basement. When she saw Cade in his enclosed play area, she exclaimed, "Hi Cade, I'm Sarah! Oh, my goodness, he is so cute! Lila told me I'd fall in love with him, but I had no idea he was so small and adorable!" I already liked Sarah and I sensed Cade did too. Going forward, I felt at ease that he was in good hands.

Sarah climbed into the play area and asked me to put the nearby children's table and two little chairs into the enclosure. She asked for certain types of toys and Cade's preferred snacks. When they'd be working, and I was upstairs, I'd hear Sarah clapping and cheering for Cade after he had done something successfully. The first few sessions went well since her intention was to get Cade comfortable with her and establish a friendly relationship. But after those first few sessions, along with the cheers I heard a lot of Cade's screaming tantrums and protests. From upstairs I heard Sarah repeat phrases such as "oh well," "too bad" and "no thanks" firmly but kindly and with intent to clearly express indifference. All the while, Cade would be having a meltdown. Unlike what I imagine most parents would feel, I didn't care that Cade was having a miserable time if that meant he was getting "fixed." In fact, the more he fought against Sarah, the more I felt she was correcting his problems, kind of like a detox. Sometimes I'd come downstairs to check on Sarah and Cade to see if I could get an update on how things were going. It didn't take much effort on Sarah's part to convince me to never, *ever* come down to the basement when Cade was in the middle of a tantrum. Sarah was very adamant about this because she explained that I would be re-enforcing his bad behavior by coming to the rescue. Cade would learn that all he had to do to get Mommy or get out of an unfavorable situation with Sarah was to have a meltdown. I would be permitted to enter the room only when Cade was quiet and calm. James, on the other hand, had more of a challenge following Sarah's strict rules. She would often scold, yes, scold James about interfering with Cade's learning, thus setting Cade back into bad habits. James' heart was in the right place as he was just worried for his little buddy. He would worry that Cade was hurt or getting hurt. Not me, I trusted Sarah and her bold methods. I would've let her slap the autism right out of him if it had been possible. I've always been a big believer of tough love. I think in some cases, tough love with a compassionate purpose makes for great parenting – particularly when dealing with a child with special needs. If a parent believes their child has greater potential to live a more normal life, then that parent has no other option than to push the child as far as possible without going over the boundary of what is appropriate. It's a tough balance to strike!

Before Sarah left after the end of each session, she'd give me the scoop. Some days, we'd end-up talking for an hour at the front door after she had already put on her jacket. Sarah's heart was totally committed to Cade's success, I could tell. She would tell me all the things he did well and the things with which he struggled. Mostly, I would complain to Sarah about the issues I had had in public with Cade when she wasn't around. I would tell her about occasions where I had followed her advice and what the outcome was. Did I do the right thing? I'd tell her about my feelings of frustration and desperation. She listened but never offered sympathy. Sometimes she'd say something to make me feel empowered like, "Very good! You did it right."

Sarah could tell whether or not I'd been following her advice. It was evident during her sessions with Cade. She would often ask me what we'd been doing at home to redirect certain behaviors, and then she would reiterate the right way with a scolding undertone. I feared Sarah a bit, but I respected her a lot more. I hated disappointing her, and I worked very hard to learn my role. Sarah explained passionately that most of the child's learning comes from Mom and Dad, not the therapist.

I was beginning to relate to the story of musical artist, Ray Charles. Ray Charles was a very young boy who was raised in a very poor household when he and his family learned that he would soon lose his sight due to glaucoma, which he eventually did at the tender age of seven. His desperate mother knew she could do absolutely nothing to improve his medical situation, so she implemented her version of tough love to prepare him for his new life-to-be. She would not come to his aid when his deteriorating sight would prevent him from finding a lost or fallen object. It's been said that Ray Charles' mother would sit back and quietly watch her son do the basic things that we, the sighted, take for granted. Though he would struggle terribly, I imagine that it was torture for her not to intervene. I believe that his mother knew that if she did, he would forever be dependent on others to get through life. Not only did he become independent, but obviously, very talented, wealthy and famous. I know how his mother must have felt, and her story really inspired me to persevere and be a better mother to Cade. And it was Sarah who gave me the tools to do just that.

Sarah always reminded me to never let Cade win the battle. I needed to be two steps ahead and fight hard now, because if I didn't, I'd someday have a strong male adult child who wouldn't be so easy to correct. Sarah had said things to me that tattooed a warning onto my brain. She said, "Do you want to deal with Cade's tantrums when he's eighteen? If you're having a hard time now, what do you think it'll be like when he's an eighteen-year-old man who is bigger and stronger than you?" Sarah and I paused as I shuddered at the thought.

"Well maybe he'll outgrow it," I said clinging to any shred of hope.

"Maybe, but are you willing to take that chance?" she asked.

"Hell no," I replied, appalled at the idea.

"Well, I suggest you take what I'm telling you very seriously." Sarah was never afraid of putting James and I in our place. Today, I am grateful to her for that, but I was more annoyed than grateful back then.

Cade turned two in the New Year, and he was well into the new therapy routine. I hated being home during the day, so outings were commonly taken throughout the week. When James was at work and Cade didn't have therapy, Cade and I would go out to the mall or somewhere enclosed because the weather in January was not ideal for a long walk outdoors. I would have liked to go more often than we did but each time we'd go, a tantrum would ensue. I felt somewhat better equipped now that I had the tactics I had gained from Sarah – it was implementing them that was the tricky part. But I had a bit more confidence to tackle any Cade-induced chaos now. Cade was walking well by this time, but he loved being pushed in his stroller. I would try to make the mall experience as pleasant as possible for him by making his favorite snacks accessible to him the entire length of the visit. I'd put rice puffs, rice cakes or Chex cereal in the tray in front of him, and I'd check on him every so often to make sure he was stocked. Cade had not yet tried ice cream, or any unhealthy mall treat because I was waiting for him to express interest in trying those things before exposing him to them. To this day, he still rejects almost all sweets... *Yay!* Cade savored his snacks at a slow and steady pace with much enjoyment. I'd take him to the toy store and we'd play a little, but he'd barely show any interest. There would always be a Thomas the Tank Engine display where kids could go and play with the trains on a wooden track. I fretted whenever there were other children around because I knew I'd have to apologize to a parent for Cade's aggressive behavior toward their child. Of course, I did everything I could to redirect Cade from snatching trains out of the hands of little strangers, but I wasn't always successful. I would give the toy back to the child and I would apologize on his behalf since he was not yet able to verbalize. Even if he was able, Cade had zero social awareness and he wouldn't have understood what he'd done wrong anyway. Cade never cared to engage with the other children because, to him, they were merely obstacles in his way. He never looked at a child's face or into a child's eyes. When he would be asked to engage in play, he would ignore them. I always had to interject with an explanation of some sort, and I would emulate what ought to have been Cade's replies by speaking on his behalf. After I'd return the toy to the child, Cade would have a meltdown... a bad one. That would force me to pack-up and get out. The crazy thing is, instead of avoiding that situation altogether, I would go to the same toy store every couple of weeks and repeat it all again expecting a better result. That's what Sarah would urge me to do. I felt like I was going mad like a demented lab-rat that kept getting zapped repeatedly expecting to get the cheese. Sarah gave me hope that I just might eventually get that cheese if I just kept trying.

Just like when we went to the supermarket, when we would walk around the mall, I would sometimes go back a few steps because something might have grabbed my attention. Cade would go off the wall! He would slam his head back in the stroller and wail. Rage would develop from there and it would involve biting the stroller like a rabid, wild dog, kicking and squirming out of his seat onto the floor in protest. I feared for his safety because he would flail his head about, and nothing would stop him from smashing his head on the concrete floor. I remember being amazed by the veins that would pop out of his neck and forehead as he'd clamp his jaws shut while trying to get bursts of screams out at the same time. His face would turn bright red and he'd perspire so much that his clothes would become hot and damp. It seemed like his body was possessed by something out of The Exorcist. The height of Cade's tantrums would fluctuate throughout the next two hours. Exhaustion would bring him down to the point where I thought it would be over, but seconds later it would start-up again as before. I'd remember Sarah's advice to never react to his behavior. I had to stay cool, calm, and totally indifferent to his outbursts though it was eating me up inside. All the while, store clerks would exit their stores to see what all the commotion was about, and mall patrons would pass with snide remarks and dirty looks. Very few passers-by were friendly and sympathetic, while most ignored us. I remember often crying silently under my sunglasses and feeling devastatingly defeated.

I would regularly call James on my cell phone from my car in the parking lot while he was at work, and I'd vent out my frustrations and anger to him about how difficult it all was, while crying. I'd tell him horrible things about how I hated being home with Cade and how unfair it was that I had to face these unbelievable challenges all by myself. I'd tell him how resentful I was that he was at work. James was always very sympathetic and understanding of my feelings. He'd refuel me with positive words of encouragement like, "Cade is the luckiest boy in the world to have you as his mommy."

It is so important for parents to learn from their child's therapists, or at least, research ABA (Applied Behavior Analysis). Understand how your child learns best so that you can help them. Adopt a new habit of applying ABA everywhere you and your child go. It will be difficult, but you are not alone! And, the investment of your efforts will pay back enormously for a lifetime.

CHAPTER 5

THE CHALLENGES WE FACE WHEN NOTICING THE GAINS OF OTHER CHILDREN

The following spring, Cade became eligible for government funding for twenty-five hours a week of therapy for an indefinite amount of time. I felt really torn by this news. On one hand, I was grateful to the taxpayer for affording Cade the ability to get all the help he needed (and some), and on the other hand, we couldn't just accept fewer hours – we had to take the full twenty-five hours per week, or the deal was off. After talking with James and my parents, we decided to move forward with the government's offer. My parents were never really informed of the severity of Cade's diagnosis, but I told them that no one could deny that he needed help. Autism or no autism, Cade needed some intervention. My mom put the proposed plan into perspective for me by explaining that nothing's set in stone. If further therapy didn't benefit Cade and we wanted to quit down the road, we'd quit. We didn't want to regret turning away from this opportunity without at least trying it. James and I were mortified by the idea of giving up so much of our private lives to the therapists who'd be walking through our doors. We were also concerned for Cade, as twenty-five hours seemed exhaustive. I expressed my unease to Sarah about our privacy and about Cade's ability to handle the new schedule. She confirmed that my apprehension was totally justifiable and warranted. Then she told me that *playing* was a big part of therapy, and it could include outings. It sounded a bit more appealing to hear that Cade would not have to be confined indoors the whole time. Also, it turned out that Cade was just about the last child to receive funding in his age bracket in Ontario. Funding for Applied Behavioral Analysis (ABA) therapy or Intensive Behavioral Intervention (IBI) therapy had been recently withdrawn from a specific category of kids, and was given to another group who, prior to then, were not entitled. Sounds as incomprehensible to me now as it did then! Anyway, realizing that this was truly a gift that should not be tossed aside for reconsideration, Cade began his therapy immediately.

Our family became very friendly with the handful of women who came through our doors. They were all therapists working under Lila's supervision. Except for Sarah who was in her early thirties, they were mostly in their early twenties, and Cade liked them all. They were in love with him... he was the baby of all their clients. Cade's most familiar therapists were Sarah (of course), Amanda (an adorable blonde who was famous in our house for her warm hugs), and Cindy (a free-spirited and easy-going college student whose tickles were greatly enjoyed by Cade). There were others we got to know along the way, but these girls were the main faces. James and I got to love them all and I think they grew to love our family too. I believe that these girls sparked the Casanova-like personality inside Cade because, to this day, he loves the ladies and they *love* him. For the most part, the new therapy schedule was going well, and James and I began to feel at ease.

In late May of 2005, my little Nève was born. She wasn't really little, though. At nine pounds and four ounces, she too was born by caesarean section. I had the same birthing scenario with her as I did with Cade – she was too big to fit through my pelvis. Cade wasn't very receptive to her, in fact, I don't believe he knew that she even existed for the first few months! I'd try to get Cade to touch her and I'd repeat the words, "Cade's sister, Nève." He would just pull away and go toward something more interesting. Nève was a noisy baby and Cade totally withdrew from her.

Nève had many similarities to Cade as a baby, but also many differences. As a baby, Nève also ate well and slept well for the first couple of weeks. She had a ton of dark hair and she was fat! Her face was so chubby you couldn't see her eyes for the first week. Nève had a single slit that ran across her face where her eyes were. This made us all giggle. Like Cade, she was very loud and fussy. She was never satisfied with anything and she cried about everything. Nève, however, was very alert and aware of her surroundings, and she demanded attention constantly. After the first month of trying to juggle the opposite needs of both kids, my mom felt compelled to interject with an opinion. "Tania, this is only going to get more difficult for you as the kids get older. I think you should consider getting a live-in nanny at the house to help you with Nève."

"I don't want anyone else in my house!" I firmly proclaimed. "I already have a hundred therapists here every week and I don't need a stranger living here on top of it!" I argued. "I can handle this."

About a month later, I folded. We got a live-in caregiver. The added financial responsibility to our family budget would definitely be burdensome, but I knew that my mom was right. When my mother gets an idea in her mind that she thinks will certainly improve my life or that of my brother, she will become determined to get her way. With loving intention, my mom could be extremely persuasive (maybe a bit pushy at times).

Our nanny was called Rowena. She was a newcomer to Canada from the Philippines, and her English was conversational at best. Rowena was slim and pretty with long black hair and a coffee-stain-like birthmark on her cheek that I like to call her *angel kiss*. My kids have *angel kisses* too, and I like to believe they got them when they were kissed while in the womb by energies (or angels) who love them, thus, leaving a mark.

She seemed slightly cold at first, maybe because she was shy and felt unsure about living with a new family. But it took no time before she came out of her shell. She quickly became attached to both Cade and Nève and I saw how she interacted so tenderly with them. Rowena was attentive to our needs, and whenever I seemed to be struggling with the kids, she always jumped in to help. Rowena was two years younger than me, and around that time, I was yet to turn thirty. I respected this woman's courage for leaving everything she knew and loved behind, hoping to make a better life for herself.

***

Cade was now two and a half and was still unable to communicate. However, he did gain a few more words to label what he saw, but his speech was all over the place. He had a lot of trouble producing from his mouth the sounds that he heard. Cade had such difficulty making the connection from his ears to his mouth that almost every letter and sound came out completely wrong. Even I, as his mother, could not understand most of what he was saying. For example, in German they make a sound that we don't use in English whereby an "H" sound is made closer to the front of the mouth, found in German words like "Ich" and "Dich." Weeks went by before I recognized that Cade had learned the word "fish" because he kept referring to pictures of fish as "weh-ch" pronounced with the German H sound! It became more apparent every day that though Cade could hear (according to the two hearing test results), he could not listen. I believe he has a defect in his brain that may or may not be linked to his autism that makes it extremely challenging for him to process what he hears. This was a problem that hearing aids would not be able to remedy. I was beginning to understand why his ability to acquire speech was so labored. Over time, Cade started making the connection from ears to mouth within his brain. I tried to correct Cade similarly to how Helen Keller's teacher, Anne Sullivan, would address a speech problem. I'd let Cade feel my mouth as I said a word. I later noticed that all Cade needed to fix that problem was for me to exaggerate the word repeatedly while he watched my mouth. I remember how he giggled the first time when he discovered that he had been saying a word wrong and then discovering the correct way of articulating the word. It brought him great satisfaction. His priceless reaction lit a spark of hope inside me. It was as though his little buried soul peeked out for a moment through his eyes to say, "Hi, Mom, I'm here and I'm smart." That was a big moment for him and me.

Because there was always a word to correct, Cade would often become angry and frustrated with Sarah, James and me. We all understood that this was the key to helping Cade talk. Cade lashed out with a tantrum almost every time, but that ended-up becoming rarer as he started to understand that his tantrums were getting him nowhere with us. Although our constant correcting was a nuisance to him, I think Cade gained pride in knowing that the score of words he did know, he could finally say properly.

Panic set in when it dawned on me that kids at Cade's age were eating normal foods and he was still eating pureed foods or his cereal-type snacks. Cade had all his teeth, but he never showed any interest or desire to try big-boy food. I already had a new baby and felt like Cade needed to start growing-up. In the past, I'd tried to introduce all kinds of solids at meal times, like meat, poultry, veggies, pasta and rice, but he rejected them all. It didn't seem reasonable for him to continue like this. So, I felt I had no choice but to play bad cop and lay down the new law. At meal times, I would prepare his preferred pureed foods and I'd add rice to it. When Cade realized that his food had a texture, he'd spit it out. I'd try again and again with no success. I even tried waiting a couple of hours to get him really hungry, but his intolerance for the texture was greater than his desire for food. A couple of days passed, and we were getting nowhere. I thought, *No more nonsense! This is ridiculous!* At lunch, I prepared the rice and puree mixture. When Cade saw it, he tightened his lips and tried to push the bowl away. I took a small spoonful with one hand as my other hand held down his arms. He fought fiercely against me, but my will to correct this situation was more powerful. I forcefully slid half a spoonful of food through his pinched lips, carefully avoiding hurting him as he moved his head and squirmed. Before he could spit anything out, I immediately inserted a Chex morsel into his mouth and followed it up by applauding and cheering. It surprised me that although Cade was whining with a grimacing look of disgust on his face, the great reward he received was distracting or pleasing enough that he managed to chew and swallow the food. I repeated every step at every meal for weeks. I would change and add new foods as I weaned him away from the puree completely. Also, during that time, I would remove the Chex and bring different distractions to the table such as alphabet letter cut-outs, and I'd sing alphabet songs while grasping to find the mentioned letter somewhere scattered on the table. I'd use picture books and plush toys to distract him with every bite. Teaching Cade to eat solid food was quite an event, which, of course, paid off. Finally, I managed to wean him from all distractions until he was able to eat a fairly sizable variety of foods independently. I will always remember the sweaty armpit rings I'd produce at the end of every meal.

No experience was more rewarding to me than seeing the little milestones Cade climbed and conquered. Every behavior alteration, word spoken, or any tiny sign of progress was enormous to the whole family. I often called my mom with news of some little thing Cade did that was successful. He continued appropriately labelling objects, but he was years away from forming an opinion or stating a need in a short and proper sentence. He was quickly approaching the age of three, and after months of training with the therapists, Cade had acquired the skill of pointing and reciting "I want apple" or "I want book." This was the beginning of Cade's capacity to finally communicate. At this point in Cade's life, those words were merely rote, and he didn't yet really understand the purpose of the words "I want." Yet, I was overjoyed to hear him say a series of words in a sentence like *I want this,* and *I want that.* But that feeling of being overjoyed was eventually clouded when I realized that that was all he could say for a very long time. I hardly considered that communicating. I longed to hear him say things that were more natural and normal like, "I feel tired" and "Daddy's funny." Again, the concept of "I want" was so foreign and abstract to Cade that he began using it inappropriately at the beginning of every statement. He'd say, "I want hungry" instead of "I am hungry." When he'd hear a barking dog or the doorbell, he would say "I want dog" and "I want doorbell" instead of "I hear a dog" or "I hear a doorbell." It became upsetting when "I want" was put in front of the labelled objects without actually wanting the objects. Sarah tried to teach Cade the meaning of "I want" by rewarding him with preferred treats and toys when he would use the term correctly, like "I want Chex." Sarah would repeat this exercise again and again until Cade had mastered the meaning, understanding, and consequence of this demand. Weeks later, another monkey-wrench would be thrown at us. Cade would develop an obsessive, bad habit known to therapists as a "stim." My assumption is that it relates to the word "stimulation." Cade suddenly started stuttering his sentences that began with "I want." It would always be the same rhythm and cadence or intonation each time, "I wah, wah, wah, wah... I want Chex," "I wah, wah, wah, wah.... I want book." It seemed to take forever for him to get his point across. James and I worked tirelessly with Cade to try and correct his speech. He hated being corrected and usually lashed out violently.

As Nève grew, I came to recognize that the milestones Cade had reached could have come so effortlessly had he not had autism. Nève transitioned from stage to stage with such ease and little, if any, effort on my part. One day as I was preparing dinner in the kitchen, both children were sitting in their highchairs eating snacks. Nève was eating cereal bits and Cade had some apple slices. At the age of eight or nine months, Nève commanded, "I want apple, I want apple!" My jaw nearly hit the floor! I called my mother with the feeling of elation, "Nève said *I want apple*! Can you believe it?" My elation quickly changed to pain as I began crying to my mom over the phone.

"Why are you crying?" she asked compassionately.

"I'm so happy for Nève, she's amazing, but this just demonstrates how very behind Cade is. It's killing me." As my mother always did, she talked with me for a while and I felt better about everything.

Nève was a big contrast to her brother. She was sharply aware of her surroundings and the people in her environment. She picked up on everything relating to speech and socializing very quickly. She was turning out to be a little wit, but she too was a late walker who made her first independent steps at seventeen months. What she lacked in gross motor skills, she had in the limitless gift for gab! Because she demonstrated such cognitive strengths and demanded so much attention, I worried that I would not find the balance to meet the very different needs of each child equally. To this day, I find it challenging, but it helps me to always vocalize this concern to them and let them both know individually how much they are adored and valued.

Cade was spending a lot of time with the therapists and that gave me some opportunity to focus my attention on Nève. While Rowena was at home with Cade and the therapist, I would sneak out with Nève to a music program for kids for an hour. She loved interacting with other children, unlike her brother. The comparison between Nève and Cade was like night and day. Nève was enthusiastic about following instructions and playing along. I felt some guilt about how much I enjoyed the normalcy of my social experiences with her, which I hadn't been able to experience with Cade.

Bravely, I enrolled Cade into Gymboree again because I knew it was terribly important for him to get used to being around other children. I hoped that this time would be different. We were now in the older program. Since so much time had passed, I thought I'd give it another try in the hope that he would be more receptive. I signed-up on the condition that I could pay for the first few classes individually. I just wanted to see how he would respond before I committed to paying for the entire series. They remembered Cade's tantrums from the previous year, so the receptionist was happy to accommodate my request. The first class was quite tough and so was the next. Cade wandered a lot, clearly disinterested in the environment of the playroom and obsessively focusing his attention on other things not pertaining to the program. He was unable to follow instructions without my total assistance. I treated the program like a glorified therapy session. I made him do everything that the others were doing. The program instructor said, "Clap your hands like this three times," and then she demonstrated, and the other children independently acted in response. With Cade, everything was hand-over-hand. I had to maneuver his feet for marching. I would exaggerate each of my own stomps with the deepest wish that he would just *see* me. It was as if he understood nothing, and it was devastating. Cade stood out from the rest. He never spoke or repeated the words back. I felt crushed by his lack of awareness and I became more and more frustrated. It was as if he was in his own world and his daily experiences happened in the matrix of his own mind, not the world in which you and I exist. He didn't want to come out.

I was the one who participated in the group for the both of us. I was loud and very animated. The bigger and louder I appeared to Cade meant there was a higher chance that I would see the tiniest glimmer of awareness – and that glimmer was invaluable to me. The physical demands of the program left me sweaty and exhausted after every class. I ended up paying for the entire program because Cade was able to tolerate the sessions and I was able to manage him. There were small segments of the program that he actually liked. Cade liked the singing parts. The instructor would take out a hand-puppet named Gymbo the Clown who was the program's mascot. Gymbo would sing his usual songs that Cade really enjoyed. Instead of singing along, Cade would emit this high-pitched tone. I figured out that that meant he was happy. It was weird, but cute.

No class had been completely tantrum-free, but I was better able to redirect Cade when I sensed him beginning to get antsy. I learned through trial and error how to shift his attention from something that might set him off to something intriguing. I'd witnessed Sarah do it throughout her interactions with Cade more than a hundred times. After pushing Cade to sit through something undesirable or tedious for a period of time, not a second before he started showing anxiety she would hand him his favorite toy or book. I would use redirection almost to the point of mastery.

During one of the last classes, Cade was being exceptionally fussy and uncooperative. I was getting impatient with him and that led him into a giant tantrum. He screamed uncontrollably, banging his head on the matted floor, his jaws clamping down on his new shirt, tearing it with his teeth. I firmly clasped him under the arms and pulled him toward the door to take him to the hallway. As we exited the doorway, Cade grabbed the frame with all his strength. I had to yank him away to close the door. The other parents watched in horror. We stayed in the hallway for about twenty minutes. He continued screaming, biting and kicking. I watched the rest of the class continue through the glass wall. The parents and children were happy and playful, but they seemed a bit uncomfortable about what they could see and hear behind the glass. The instructor had the attention of all the kids while they sang and clapped to the music. I wanted so much to have that with Cade. She sat everyone down for a short story, but the noise Cade was making behind the glass was becoming disruptive and I was feeling embarrassed. I looked down at him on the floor and I knew that we had to leave because he just wasn't going to stop before the class was over. So, I left him in the hall and I went back into the class to get my purse. The instructor stopped reading and asked, "Is he okay?"

The only words that came out as I broke down in tears were, "He has autism."

That was the first time I ever said it in public. It felt like a dagger through my chest. I quickly rubbed my eyes dry, gathered my things, and left. I lifted Cade over my shoulder and carried him out of the building. I don't remember if I ever took him back there.

***

Many months went by, maybe he was already three, and it was obvious that Cade's speech and communication was still the most delayed and severely under-developed learned skill. He had no difficulty learning more individual words (mostly nouns for labelling), he knew hundreds of them, but he was unable to combine them to make a simple statement. It seemed almost impossible for Cade to change thoughts into sentences. He continued to reach some small milestones when working with the therapists, and that was encouraging, but I never remember feeling gratitude for those milestones. I only remember feeling bitter toward God for putting our family in this position in the first place, and I was angry. My anger and bitterness always triumphed over the positive gains Cade was making. James was always trying to explain to me that those feelings were toxic and dangerous to Cade's growth. I was so engulfed by fear and negative emotions that I was incapable of comprehending James' warnings. My resentment toward James was quietly breeding internally as he refused to share my pain. His outlook on Cade's future was always positive and, I thought, unrealistically confident. How did *he* know Cade was going to be fine! James claimed that he had developed some psychic ability in the former years of our marriage, but I wasn't totally convinced. It's not that I didn't trust him or believe him, but I had purposefully removed myself from his new-found state of enlightenment and spiritual growth. I wasn't psychologically or emotionally prepared to accept these changes in my husband. I was quite satisfied with the guy I married who wasn't all "in touch with the universe." As James evolved on this journey of self-discovery and inner peace, I felt like I was left behind, unable to remove myself from the darkness that had swallowed me. We carried opposite energies. James was positive, and I was negative. This is where our marriage struggled. While James was trying to nurture goodness, positivity and gratitude into our family life, I was under a black cloud which blocked the sun, and my attention was on all that was wrong with *everything* and *everyone*.

I hated how peaceful he appeared about Cade's autism. James was very patient with me and he remained my number one cheerleader. I know James understood that the pain I was dealing with was something only I could sort out. In the meantime, he prayed to God a lot and was regularly giving Him thanks. I, on the other hand, told God that I was upset with Him for doing this to my child who I loved so much. How could He give me such a beautiful and, otherwise, healthy little boy, and do this to him. I was very conflicted about how I felt toward Him. God was a friend that I was very angry with and didn't really want to talk to. Meanwhile, James was becoming God's BFF.

Cade surprised us when he learned to use the toilet after only two-days of training with Sarah. We expected the worst and got the best. This was a very welcomed change from the usual scenario where Cade's learning had always been laborious and complicated. However, Cade was trailing behind the average child in every way except his advanced fine-motor skills. Sarah had come to the realization that Cade had grasped the skill of drawing very quickly.

As part of one of his therapy sessions, Sarah would create a simple drawing, like a flower, on one side of a chalk board and he'd have to duplicate it on the other side. Cade mastered this skill immediately, and we were all ecstatic. It turned out that he was very advanced in that department. Before long, Cade was drawing tens of detailed pictures a day. He drew constantly during his free time. Cade's subjects often came from the characters he watched on his favorite DVDs. He would obsessively devote hours drawing the same kinds of pictures. He must have made a thousand drawings of Elmo in Elmo's World. After the Elmo fixation passed, Cade would make scores of booklets full of drawings on the letter-characters he watched on his Leap Frog DVDs. He would draw pictures that he saw in his picture books. Cade loved the Baby Einstein and Little Einstein series and he'd draw the characters from the books and DVDs. His drawing skills shocked everyone in our circle. It astounded me how this little boy had so much talent and ability in one way, and yet was so deficient in almost every other way. Cade's artistic talents gave me a good dose of hope that his future might be brighter and more fulfilling than I had expected.

He wasn't yet three years old when we made another amazing discovery. I was in the basement with Cade in the play area where he normally had therapy. There were all kinds of crafts, drawing and coloring materials there. The TV was on because Cade was watching one of his favorite shows while drawing a beautiful picture. I sat next to him enjoying the moment when I picked up a blue pen and began to write something down. I don't remember why or to whom I was writing, but I remember writing the word *blue*. Cade looked over my shoulder and said, "Blue." I was a bit stunned, but my rationality set in – it was in blue inked pen after all. So, I wrote *red*. Cade said, "Red." Now I was getting excited. I then began to pick up the pace and wrote down every color of the rainbow, every farm and zoo animal, and every transportation vehicle that I could think of. Without a moment of hesitation, Cade read them all. *CADE COULD READ?!*

I frantically grabbed the phone and started to call everyone, "Cade can read!" It seemed like a miraculous occurrence since no one had even attempted to teach him. I ran back to him and grabbed a few of his books that he had lying around. As I briefly looked through them, Cade approached me. He pointed to the page I had opened, and he read the word *CAT*. This particular book was a hard board book made for toddlers. When open, the left page had a picture or photo of an animal and the right page had the written word of the animal. We had about a million books like this on our shelves, all with different subjects like transportation, colors, numbers, letters, animals, etc.

Today, we believe that Cade learned to read by memorizing or recognizing what a word *looked* like rather than sounding it out like most of us do when learning to read. Cade saw the picture of a cat and recognized that the symbols (or letters) associated with that animal looked like this: C A T. And the symbols representing the picture of a dog looked like this: D O G. And since Cade had mastered the ability to verbally label almost every noun, he knew to say the words that he was seeing. I assume this is how people learn to read other languages like Chinese and Japanese, whereby many of the small words are represented by a single symbol rather than reading a word based on phonetics, like in English and other languages that follow the Greek alphabet. Currently, Cade is a near flawless speller because of the way he learned to read. He has never misspelled the words *would, could, should, cough, laugh...* because he has never relied on the phonetics of words to get by. Cade memorizes the *appearance* of a word with his photographic mind. Some intellectually average children find it easier to learn the same way as Cade. Some parents choose to use flash cards to teach their kids to read so that the child memorizes the appearance of a word rather than sounding it out. Most parents find that relying on phonetics can be confusing and contradictory to the basic rules of reading when teaching their children to read.

It was during this time in Cade's life that I started to understand how we could help him most effectively. It was abundantly clear to us that Cade had unconventional intelligence, so now it was up to us to figure out how to use this skill to his advantage. Because he had great difficulty processing information through his ears, the majority of what we'd say to him, directly or indirectly, would not be processed or stored as useful information to him. I compared Cade to the Peanuts characters when they heard their teacher talk. *"Whah whah whah"* I believe is mostly what Cade heard when we spoke. So, the information Cade lacked, that would otherwise be received through the auditory sense, would be provided almost entirely by visual mechanisms. This explained how Cade taught himself to read before he could even form a proper sentence and draw at an advanced level. I realized while watching Nève grow that she, like most babies, initially grasped information that she would hear. Long before a baby recognizes the difference between red and blue or a circle and a square, they hear and learn the words *Mama and Dada.* They tend to repeat the words their parents teach them with significant ease. A year or two later is when a child begins to place the information they learn visually in their memory stores.

First comes color differentiation, animals and shapes recognition, and later comes such complexities as understanding letters and numbers. Well, Cade did it backwards; which is why we thought he was partially deaf. He started learning through his eyes and much later, through his ears. With this discovery came great opportunity for growth.

The day we learned that Cade taught himself to read was one of the most triumphant days of my life! God had delivered me a gigantic gift that day. I remember finally feeling grateful.

Try not to feel discouraged with your child's delays. I know this is very difficult advice to accept and apply. The differences your child has compared to the children in their play group, or to their sibling(s), will be noticeable and hurtful – that's normal and to be expected. Please find real understanding and truth that your autistic child is brilliantly intelligent in their own way. They learn unconventionally, but they have real capacity to learn, develop and progress triumphantly. Remember to focus on their beautiful individuality and embrace their unique skills and interests. Push them to their fullest potential but realize that they will fight you every step of the way. Stay firm, positive and strong as you will eventually find new and rewarding growth in your child's development.

CHAPTER 6

CADE GOES TO PRESCHOOL

It was about this time when James and I returned from a week-long vacation. We went without the kids because James felt it was important to spend quality time together as a couple, and we needed to distance ourselves temporarily from the worries of home and work. My parents willingly - but nervously - offered to watch the kids at our house for the entire week. My mom felt more comfortable knowing that Rowena was around. Rowena was familiar with the children's schedules and had been regularly exposed to Cade's tantrums – and knew how to deal with them.

James and I arrived home on Sunday afternoon. My mom and dad greeted us at the door with the kids in their arms. We noticed that this time Cade wasn't angry, he was just oblivious. After the kids went off to play, my parents filled us in on what had happened in our absence.

I will never forget what happened next because for the first time since Cade's birth, I finally felt like someone understood me. As my mom gave us the details of the day-to-day events of the week, she started to cry.

"Tania, I do not envy you," my mother tearfully uttered, "It's hard what you do. It's hard." She continued, "Cade and Nève are so beautiful and I love them more than anything in this world, but you don't have it easy." My mother embraced me. I couldn't bear to see my mom crying over both Cade and me, so I tried to reassure her that I had it all under control and that I was more than able to cope with the challenges on a daily basis.

"I know you must be tired after this week," I started, "So you're probably feeling a bit emotional from that." I downplayed my mom's experience.

***

Sarah had been with us for about a year when she recommended that we place Cade in a half-day daycare program to give him more experience interacting with other children. Since he was a full year older from the first time we tried daycare, about three and a half, we thought we'd have better luck. We called many schools but, most were either fully enrolled or did not have the support staff to deal with kids like Cade. After many phone calls, a daycare agreed to do a trial run. When James and I went to consult with the school's director during school hours, we were shocked that the children were independently putting on and taking off their shoes, picking up their lunch bags, sitting nicely at their assigned seats, and eating their snacks. We couldn't even dream of seeing Cade do any of those things! James and I looked at each other discouraged and felt afraid that Cade would not be able to hold his own in this environment. We confessed to the director that Cade was light-years away from having this kind of independence. She tried to convince James and I that independence would be acquired in class. We were not so optimistic. Cade started on a Monday and by Tuesday they told us Cade had to leave. The lady in charge informed me when I was picking him up that it wasn't working out. She said he was too unsociable, he didn't play nicely with the other kids and he wasn't following any directions. Cade was too distracting to the other children. I politely thanked her for the opportunity, but I was truly crushed. I called

James, in tears as usual, and explained what had happened. He would console me lovingly and keep reminding me that there were bigger and better opportunities ahead for Cade. We explored two more schools and we were rejected both times.

James' mantra was "everything happens for a reason" and – more annoyingly – "everything's perfect." I was getting sick of hearing it! But it turned out that James was right. We ended up finding the perfect school for Cade – or so we thought. We found a school in Toronto that was a partially subsidized pre-school/ nursery school that integrated children with special needs with typical children. The special needs of those students ranged from autism, severe hearing loss, mental disabilities and physical limitations. The average kids were either from the neighborhood or a sibling to a child with special needs. I thought this school was heaven-sent for us because I knew they would be equipped to deal with Cade's tantrums, and he would be encouraged to interact with all the different children. I was so excited to have found this dream-school for Cade because I felt like it was going to help him a lot. Cade would spend the morning at pre-school, I'd pick him up at eleven-thirty and head home for lunch. He'd spend most of the rest of the day having therapy. Sometimes he would have therapy well into the evening hours.

His teachers at this well-known and respected school were Suzi and Mary, an excellent, high-energy duo. I felt they had the toughest job in the universe. Not only did they have to juggle ten kids between the ages of three and five, which in itself is exhausting, but half of them required extra attention. Some needed to be spoon-fed, or a diaper needed changing, a tantrum needed to be extinguished, or a child needed to be carried. These issues were all addressed while the teachers managed to engage the entire class with projects and activities at the same time. I was amazed by Suzi and Mary's composure at the end of the day. They seemed a bit sweaty and flushed in the face, understandably, but their voices remained cool and calm. Suzi or Mary would talk to each parent at pick-up about their child's experience, no matter how briefly. Sometimes, one of them would give me news that Cade had learned a new skill or had said something suitable to a classmate. They relished telling me about his accomplishments as much as I relished receiving them. Rarely did they give me news that Cade had behaved badly. Only if I probed them with specific questions would they tell me about anything negative. Overall, Mary and Suzi seemed to have it all under control. I felt so relieved that we found this place for Cade that a year later we enrolled Nève into the nursery program.

Nève was a rock-star student. She socialized very well and loved to play. She stayed at the school for about a year until we felt that she could use a greater challenge, so we moved her to a Montessori near James' place of work.

Cade was having such a positive and fulfilling experience at the school. He was learning to tolerate the presence of other children by sharing toys, art utensils and the general space of the small classroom. Cade loved the games and the daily visits from Wayne, a singer and guitarist. Cade was mostly interested in painting and drawing pictures, which received many compliments from the teachers and other parents.

As soon as the classroom door opened for the parents to come in and greet their kids, I'd jump in very enthusiastically and animatedly to get Cade's undivided attention. I may have gotten the attention of all the students and even the parents, but my goal was to get Cade as excited to see me as I was to see him. I wanted to set an upbeat and positive momentum to set the tone for the day, because I knew how fragile and fleeting a moment of calmness was in the world of Cade. Sometimes, that positive mood carried through until we got home, but I remember that in most cases, hell began at school dismissal despite my charismatic arrival. Sometimes, I felt like he didn't want to come home...

Cade didn't want to leave a craft or painting unfinished when the class ended. So, I would wait as long as I could for him to complete his project. After all the kids had left and Suzi and Mary were done tidying the classroom, we'd have to pry Cade away from his work which would set him off into a fit of rage. Cade would wait until we walked out into the school lobby before he would drop and sprawl himself onto the floor and refuse to get up while screaming. Since that happened a few times, the teachers promised to ensure that he was given enough time to finish his art long before dismissal.

During Cade's time at this pre-school, I learned another valuable lesson – don't be late! Not even for a millisecond! If Cade saw the other parents all entering the classroom together, and I came trailing in a minute later, he would drop and scream with fury as if to let me know that I was very wrong and that I would now be punished with a drawn-out meltdown. Mary or Suzi would sometimes take him out into the lobby so that I could collect his belongings in the class. When I'd try putting on his coat, he'd start to fight me by kicking and biting. All the while, the school director would be watching us through her open door while offering encouraging words to Cade to get up off the floor and be good for Mommy. He'd totally ignore her during the meltdown. If she was on the phone, she'd get up from her chair to shut the door. I only had so much time to wait for Cade to settle down or we'd be late for the next round of therapy lessons. After about fifteen minutes of waiting for Cade to settle down, I'd begin to lose my patience since I knew Sarah, Amanda or Cindy would not be happy standing at our door, waiting for us to get home. I would recount the advice Sarah had given me about being indifferent to Cade and his behaviors, and try to act like nothing unpleasant was going on. So, I'd physically bring him to his feet by holding him under the arms while he flailed his limbs. I'd verbally mimic Sarah, "Nice standing, Cade," which would further ignite his anger. Then I would continue with, "Let's walk... nice walking, Cade." He would drag his legs all the way to the car while screaming wildly. Because the school was in the heart of the city, parking was a luxury, and the very few spots the school had were reserved for building employees only. Parents had to park their cars along the main street with the hazard lights flashing. The traffic police often looked the other way, aware of the complexities of the situation. When Cade and I (and sometimes Nève) got to the car, I had to put him down on the sidewalk to get my keys. The sidewalk would be wet from snow or slush, so I had to be quick. I also feared the busy traffic that zoomed just feet away from us. The next challenge I faced was getting Cade into the car and buckled into his car seat safely. I think that was the hardest part of it all. Cade was so powerful and ferocious that I had to use all my physical strength to lock him down into his seat. On a good day this would take ten minutes, but on a day like this one, our rigid schedule would become much delayed. I'd call home to let Rowena know and ask her to make a sandwich for Cade so that he could eat quickly. Before calling Rowena, I would call my husband – my best friend and lifeline. I would emotionally collapse while purging to him what had just happened, and as I did so Cade would continue to tantrum violently in the back seat unaware of my rant on the phone. If Nève was there too, Cade's behavior would cause her to cry as well. Sometimes, Cade even managed to squirm out of the tightened straps of his car seat. I would have to turn onto a side road before I could stop the car and start the fight with him all over again.

After witnessing this spectacle nearly three times a week at dismissals, the school director, Mrs. S, called me into her office for a chat one afternoon. Mrs. S. was a really nice older lady who always seemed positive, supportive, and very helpful to me and the other parents. First, she expressed her delight with Cade's progress in class and how he was making great learning strides. I frequently extended my sincere gratitude to her and the staff of this school for the opportunities they had given Cade and our family. As we spoke, the tone of the conversation became more serious. Mrs. S. explained her concerns regarding the way I'd take Cade out to the car. She assured me that it wasn't her personal opinion, but my actions could be interpreted as being abusive from the perspective of people on the outside. I could not believe what I was being told! Then, Mrs. S. gently offered her unfavorable opinion of the practice of ABA therapy, and how some believed it to be too aggressive. I felt like I'd been sucker-punched in the stomach. I told her that I didn't care what other people thought in this overly sensitive society! I had to get Cade out of the school and into the car somehow... any suggestions?! If I had an abusive mindset, I would have beaten the hell out of Cade by now! But I hadn't so much as raised a hand to him thus far. Believe me, there were many, many times I fantasized about giving him a big slap, but I understood that that would be detrimental.

After taking a day to process what Mrs. S. had said, I attempted the impossible by trying to be more discrete with my ways, before realizing that it just wasn't possible. Maybe if I'd knocked him out with a two-by-four, and THEN dragged him out, I'd appear more discrete. DISCLAIMER: I'm joking!

It took a while, but those behaviors became much less frequent and less intense as the months went on, and I attributed that to the ABA approach Mrs. S frowned upon. I was better able to manage, anticipate and prevent Cade's outbursts for the most part. Mrs. S. and some of the staff acknowledged the improved changes in Cade's behavior as far as dismissal went. Unfortunately, that wasn't the last of our troubles at this school.

On an upbeat note, Cade had his first birthday party at our house that included all his classmates. Previously, we never really did much to celebrate his birthdays except have my brother, his wife and my parents over for cake. Sadly, James' family are all scattered across the US, so their presence is a rare occasion. Cade had never been in a pre-school program long enough to make any friends, and Cade and Nève didn't have any cousins in Canada yet. So, it was really fun and exciting to throw Cade a Wiggles themed party for his fourth birthday. I spent weeks making life-size cardboard cut-outs of the characters. We hid all that from Cade. We bought dozens of floating colorful balloons to fill the space, and James dressed-up as Captain Feathersword (he looked amazingly like him!). Wiggles' music played loudly, and we had Wiggles-themed food and games. When Cade saw it all initially, he went ballistic. Cade truly came out of his shell for the first time to my family. He danced and ran around like he had ants in his pants! He seemed so overjoyed it was a blessing to watch him experience this breakthrough. Cade was not very interactive with his guests, but everyone had a blast! Thanks to my brother, Nève had her first taste of potato chips and sweets. She got hooked for life! (Great...) After the party, we agreed that we should do this type of thing every year for the kids' birthdays. For Cade, it seemed therapeutic and healthy. We figured that if we exposed Cade to more big presentations of things he loves and knows, the more aware he will become of his surroundings. So, James and I took the kids to two Wiggles concerts and a handful of Disney on Ice shows. We started taking them to kids' movies – even 3D movies. The crowds were a bit overwhelming for Cade at the beginning, but James kept him closely to block from him some of the crowd's energy. Eventually, that was a sensitivity that Cade overcame. We would see a side of Cade that we'd not be able to tap into otherwise – just like when I used to sing to him when he was a baby and make loud, vibrant sounds and gestures to gain his focus.

Things seemed to be going well for a while until the latter part of Cade's second year at pre-school. Cade started biting other students. On two separate occasions he bit so hard that he almost broke skin and the teachers had to report it to the office. They take these matters very seriously. Because Cade had almost no ability to communicate his feelings verbally, he would resort to communicating them physically, as you already know. When a child would yank, say, a paintbrush out of Cade's hands, he had no words to express his distress over what had just happened. His instinctive reaction was to retaliate physically, in this case, with biting. The parents of both victimized children were very understanding when Cade and I apologized. Standing before the victim-parent, I explained to Cade in a reprimanding fashion that that behavior was not going to be tolerated. I knew that it was pretty pointless to scold Cade after the incident had occurred because he didn't understand much of what I was saying anyway, I did it more for the benefit of the other parent and child. The day after he bit each kid, Cade would come to class with a small gift as a gesture of remorse. Both students were in the "typical kids" category.

I didn't want anything to jeopardize Cade's opportunity to attend this school since I believed we had no other opportunities. So, on both occurrences, I spoke to Mrs. S. apologetically. In turn, she apologized to me that the teachers did not stop Cade in time. I thought that was weird but nice. I made Mrs. S. aware of my fear that she, too, would kick us out if things continued this way. She pledged to me that Cade's standing in the school would not be affected. Again, I thanked her profusely for her compassion and understanding. Still, I felt as if we were walking on eggshells and Cade's days at this place could be numbered.

I spoke to Mary and Suzi to find out what actions they had taken immediately after the biting incidents. I learned that they did nothing. "No punishment or consequence?" I asked.

"No. Our goal is to jump in, when we can, and intercept the situation before it even happens. We just didn't catch him on time," Suzi explained. I was perplexed by this statement.

"So, how's Cade supposed to know what he did was wrong? It's too late now for me to teach him."

"Well, we don't believe in punishment here. It goes against our philosophical teaching methods."

My jaw dropped. *And this is why kids today act like spoiled nuts!*

When Sarah learned of this, she was not happy. "Great, so Cade's gonna think it's OK to bite because no one will teach him otherwise!"

"I know!" I added in full agreement.

"That totally goes against ABA," she remarked.

"I know, Sarah, but you said he needs to be in a social setting with other kids, and no other school will take him," I argued.

I promised Sarah I'd speak to Mary and Suzi about whether they'd make a small exception for Cade by including negative consequence for bad behavior. I tried to convince them that this would surely make things easier on them. To my surprise, they said they'd do the best they could. I'm not sure what that meant, but I had to stay hopeful.

As the months went on, I had more reports from Suzi or Mary that Cade had conflicts with other students, especially with the second boy he had bitten. I'll call him Aaron. In most of the cases, they were able to prevent Cade from retaliating, but it was becoming quite problematic for the high-energy duo to keep-up with Cade's reactions. Unbelievably, Cade bit Aaron again! This time it seemed more serious. I saw Aaron's mother at the school, so I apologized profusely, and reiterated Cade's problems. She seemed very sympathetic of my situation.

The next day, Mrs. S. invited me to her office. I was really nervous. "I'm sorry, Mrs. Malaniak," Mrs. S. began regretfully.

I interrupted, "You're kicking us out, right?" Mrs. S. had tears in her eyes. I could see how terrible she felt, especially since just a couple of months prior she had reassured me that Cade was not going to be kicked out. I felt really betrayed. Mrs. S. practically groveled for my forgiveness as she explained her side. I was dying inside, but to my frustration, I suppressed my emotions with a smile. I have always struggled to let people know my true feelings. I said to Mrs. S., "Aaron has a thousand schools to choose from. Cade has only this one." Mrs. S. song-and-danced her way around the conversation, giving me numbers to call and public schools to research. I wanted nothing to do with any of it.

The next day Aaron's mother called me. She must have found my number on Cade's birthday party invitation from a while back. It took everything inside me not to be rude with her. I understood that she was protecting her kid, but I would have gone to further lengths to ensure my child did not provoke or instigate a situation with a child who did not have the tools to defend himself, especially in light of the classroom dynamic. If Nève had been bitten by a child with special needs, I would have made an effort to get her to understand how to interact with that child without provoking him/her. I don't think it would have been a difficult thing for her to implement, either. Nève was never bitten by Cade because she never provoked him to do so. In this day and age, I feel that parents aren't parenting. They blame everyone else but themselves or their child.

Aaron's mom told me that she felt terrible that Cade had been expelled and that it was never her intention for that to happen. She asked me where Cade could go now. Of course, I told her honestly that I had exhausted every other option. This was the only place he had successfully attended. I didn't have a clue what we could do now. She sounded as though she felt bad, but I don't think that she lost any sleep over it. Why would she? This woman had no idea what a mother of an autistic child goes through. The staff at the school had made the wrong decision and we had to deal with the consequences.

We picked ourselves up and dusted ourselves off again. Our focus needed to be on Cade – screw everyone else.

Try to partner with educators who are on the same page as you. This will be easier to do today than it was in 2006/2007, as teachers now have more knowledge and understanding.

*We used ABA methods to minimize and eventually extinguish Cade's tantrums in the school lobby. However, the **non-existence** of ABA in the classroom resulted in the increase in Cade's retaliation behavior, and consequently his expulsion. Stay strong and consistent with the application of ABA. As I've said before, it will pay off.*

I highly recommend that you throw big, colorful parties for your children that include their favorite music and themes. Also, if your child gets invited to parties, make a real effort to get them there. This will heighten their awareness, allow more opportunity for them to engage with other kids, and your child will likely gain a lot of joy during these events, which is medicinal and therapeutic to them, and to you. The bigger the party... the bigger the reaction.

CHAPTER 7

A TYPICAL DAY OUT WITH CADE

I was sad about the constant rejection and feeling increasingly isolated from the world around me. I was exhausted from being stressed-out every waking moment and suffering from countless colds and ailments that manifested from all that stress. I was fed up of seeing how different my kid was from everyone else's. And I was sick of James telling me "everything happens for a reason" and "everything's going to be fine" while he was at work having a normal life. I regularly tormented myself with resentful thoughts and jealous feelings toward James. Aside from my annoyance about how at peace James was with Cade's situation, I envied that he got to escape eight hours a day. It seemed to me that he had the chance to get away from the problems at home, mingle with other adults, go out for lunches with associates, and take a mental break from home and kids. I never gave myself the chance to leave and take personal time to feed my own soul. It's a problem that I'm still trying to correct for myself, but at least now I am aware that I need that "me" time. I rarely left the house without the kids for the first six years of Cade's life. I was more often than not, by myself with the kids when I really needed support from James or Mom. Every time Cade got rejected, whispered about, or looked at with judgement, a bit more negativity would be stuffed into my baggage. I felt isolated and helpless having to watch my child go into fits of violence, suicidal and demonic-like states at any moment, while I had no moral support. Though Rowena was around, I didn't want her to help me tackle one of Cade's episodes, it didn't seem right. It was enough for me that she was able to whisk away little Nève and give her all the attention and comfort she needed. If it weren't for Rowena, I don't know how I would have managed.

Rowena, the kids and I used to go out together a lot. It gave me peace of mind to know that I would not be alone physically if something happened with Cade. Rowena would come along to the weekly community play groups and swim classes with me and the kids. She'd supervise Nève while I focused on Cade. Rowena would sometimes come with us to Cade's weekly homeopathic appointments. Even before Cade's formal diagnosis, we had been visiting a homeopathic / naturopathic doctor to see what remedies could be used to help control or improve his cognitive, speech and behavioral issues. I believe very strongly that alternative medicine enhanced Cade's ABA therapy. It was a painstakingly gradual process, but we learned and gained a lot over the time. The doctor we had been seeing for at least three years was Dr. Saveria (Rena) Zambri of the Canadian College of Naturopathic Medicine. I felt like we were really blessed to have found Dr. Zambri because she was a leader in her field, and I felt that Cade benefitted immensely from her expertise. Sarah frequently reported improvements after he had been administered a homeopathic remedy or supplement. We even took Sarah to a few appointments as part of the ABA session. While I talked to the doctor, Sarah would teach Cade to sit patiently, and play with toys quietly and appropriately. It was really helpful to have Sarah in the room with us because she'd offer observations about Cade's progress or regressions that I may have overlooked.

As well as homeopathy and naturopathy (which included several special diets and supplementation), James and I have tried energy work, cranial sacrum therapy, Chinese medicine, music and sound therapy, and hyperbaric therapy. All of them affected Cade in a positive way, but some more than others. We experimented with the idea that Cade's autism had manifested from a food or environmental allergy. We visited a Defeat Autism Now (DAN) doctor weekly for a year to see if Cade had sensitivities that were causing chemical and mental imbalances. We travelled to Mississauga with the family after school. At each visit to Dr. Scott Clack's office, both Cade and Nève were treated for their allergies and sensitivities with the Nambudripad's Allergy Elimination Techniques (NAET). At home one horrifying day, we discovered that Nève had a life-threatening peanut allergy. Our great desire was to lower the degree of severity to the peanut allergy reaction, and this type of therapy would help to achieve that result. We didn't find any significant allergies with Cade, but similarly to his other treatments, we enjoyed at least a small improvement whether it was related to his cognitive growth, speech development, a greater sense of awareness, or positive behavior changes.

I think James would agree that we found the most noteworthy results for Cade from homeopathy, Chinese medicine (which consisted of herbal supplementation) and hyperbaric therapy. We feel that these treatments worked well with ABA. There are a lot of charlatans in the world of alternative medicine, so if this is something you are considering, and I hope you do, please do your research to find a reputable practitioner. It can be dangerous and detrimental to work with an unqualified and inexperienced person as they could cause serious harm. In some ways, these therapies can be somewhat aggressive to a person's body, especially a child, but they can also be extremely effective. So, please find people you trust.

In the last couple of months, James has taken Cade to a woman named Eva who is an energy healer. I understand that many of you are rolling your eyes now, and that's fine, because I also rolled my eyes in the past when I'd hear the term "energy healer." A lot about me and my views have changed throughout the years. People who are very religious may say that it's the work of the devil, but the reality is that God plays the lead role in this type of healing. To an energy-healer, God is all good energy. There is no doubt that the entire galaxy is composed of different forms of energy, so even the Atheists among us who'd rather focus on the scientific aspects to energy healing should appreciate what I have to say. Quantum physics has proven that mind and thought energy can manipulate the physical world in which we live. Some people have unlocked the natural ability from their brilliant human brains to harness God's energies (or positive energy) and use it to heal ourselves and others. Supposedly, we all have brains equipped with this ability, but most of us are unknowing of this tremendous gift. The average person exercises this ability every time they have that immense feeling of love, like the love a mother has for her child. That immense feeling of love is healing and therapeutic energy for both the mother and child. One can learn to harness that "love," "energy," or "God's light" to heal oneself and others. This ability can sometimes also help to affect outcomes of events. It takes practice, time and discipline once you can get passed any skepticism. *That's* the hard part! James is developing this skill very quickly. I think it's easier for him because of his natural abilities to see, hear and feel energy, as well as having that sixth sense everyone laughs about... *'I see dead people'.*

We are always open to trying new treatments. It's great to see Cade reaping the benefits. I have spoken to a lot of parents who have tried different treatments, and if they found that the treatment didn't work as much as they had expected, they would simply stop the treatment. James and I have found that even if a small improvement is achieved, then it is beneficial to reintroduce that treatment later, so we would recommend that you keep trying and not give up. Your child may gain better results the second or third time. Also, I would not recommend long-term supplementation because it can be harsh on the child's kidneys and/or liver. Short, one to two-month spurts were enough for us to see positive changes in Cade. Then we would take a break from the supplement (such as fish oils) and reintroduce it four to six months later with renewed results that we would refer to as "bump-ups."

Over the course of Cade's life, it wouldn't be inaccurate to state that we have spent a small fortune on treatments, therapies (including speech therapy), remedies, and supplements. Honestly, if it wasn't for the financial assistance we got from my parents, we wouldn't have been able to try all the treatments the alternative medicine world has to offer. My advice to any parents facing the challenges of having an autistic child (or more than one autistic child) is to get as many family members involved in getting that child as much support as possible. Whether this is an option in your life or not, there is always hope for a brighter day. I have learned from James that the power of the mind and soul can be the strongest medicine in the world, and the deadliest poison.

At least once a week, we'd go to a local burger joint with Rowena. On one winter's day, we went to Harvey's Hamburgers for lunch. I went to the ordering counter to get the food while Rowena stayed with the kids at a nearby table. As the food was in preparation, Cade began to freak out. He was sprawled on the floor and shouting tearfully. I looked at Rowena as she tried to calm him, but he seemed so much stronger than her. I grabbed the food and rushed over to the table and I felt everyone's eyes on us. Rowena told me that he started crying because he couldn't see me. I was in the early stages of learning that when I'd leave Cade's view, if he had not been made aware of where I was going when we were in public places, he would have one of those meltdowns. It did not matter if I left his frame of vision for a fleeting second, it would set him off. Even after I had returned from the counter, the violent tantrum continued. I'd had enough of this! It must have been a difficult day for me – my patience was wearing thinner each day. I could only contain my own temper so much before I would also explode. I encouraged Rowena to start eating and asked her to keep an eye on Nève. I grabbed Cade from off the floor, shoved on his coat and took him outside. If he was going to have a tantrum, it would have to be outside. On the freezing ground, Cade struggled to tear off his coat during his fit. All that I insisted was that he kept his coat on because it was freezing and dangerous otherwise. I fought with him to keep it on, while trying to maintain an air of indifference to his bad behavior. I had accidentally left my coat in the restaurant because of the urgency. But I was sweating from dealing with Cade, so it didn't seem to matter. I welcomed the winter chill at this point. Cade and I were, literally, fighting on the ground just outside the double doors of the restaurant. Customers who'd witnessed the whole thing inside began to leave. One said to me "good luck" aloofly as he walked away. I was running out of strength and Cade was unrelenting. He'd now managed to shed his coat, and his shirt was more than halfway up his back. His fury continued as he bit down on his clothes and pulled them in a tearing motion. As a responsible mother, I couldn't allow him to be half dressed on the slushy pavement like that. I didn't need some uninformed nut calling Child Protection Services on me that day, so I opened the doors to the restaurant and told Rowena that we needed to pack up and go. I saw that she had unwrapped the burgers and laid them out invitingly as they waited for us at the table. Outside, I picked Cade up with the little strength I had left, and I "walked" him to the car like he was a marionette. I held him under the arms as he kicked, dragged his feet and bit me. Cade screamed and kicked as I forced him into the minivan. From an observer's prospective, it must have looked like I was kidnapping some random kid. Tears streamed down my face as I applied all my power to strap him down into his car seat. Though I was at the brink of cracking earlier on in this ordeal, it was at that very moment that I broke. I screamed into Cade's face, "Why are you doing this to me? Stop it! Stop it!" I didn't care who was watching me or what they were thinking. I needed to get home and Cade needed to be in his car seat. Rowena finally arrived with our bagged food, my coat, tote bags and Nève in her arms. I apologized to her for the abrupt ending to our outing, but she was very understanding – and more so – concerned.

During the short summer seasons, we tried to spend as much time outside as possible. I'd buy season passes for two out of the three amusement parks that were in our area. It's quite remarkable to have the fortune of living nearby three amusement parks when most people in North America would be lucky to live by one! I would get a season pass to Canada's Wonderland, a huge theme park that is comparable to Six Flags Great Adventure. We also got one for Ontario Place which was not as thrilling or impressive as Canada's Wonderland, but still a really fun way to spend the day with the kids who were pre-school aged then (it closed down in 2011). The third park that we visited less frequently was Centerville at Toronto Island which required a ferry ride to get to. They didn't offer season passes. Centerville catered to very young children and I loved getting away from the hubbub of the city to go there. We would also purchase yearly passes for Toronto Zoo. Although there were several other things to do nearby, the kids and I spent a big part of our summers going to these places during the week, in spite of the lengthy hours of therapy Cade had to do. I would organize the week according to the weather forecast. Sometimes therapy involved visiting one of these locations, so it worked well. Part of the therapy was to teach Cade how to behave in public places, such as how to wait in line, interact with others, and basically how to be a regular kid in a social and public environment. We saw it as a great opportunity for Cade to use the skills he'd learned, and it was a nice treat from the usual one-to-one setting in the confines of his therapy room. There were enough freezing and rainy months in the year where we'd get our fill of indoor therapy days.

Sarah has a petite stature which meant that she was able to go on all the children's rides with Cade since she was less than five feet tall. They didn't allow taller people on these rides as they were intended for young children only. Because Cade lacked awareness and the ability to comprehend reasoning and instruction, I didn't feel comfortable having him go on any rides alone as I worried he would purposefully do something dangerous to himself or to his sister, or even have a tantrum on the ride. It turned out that he was most calm on the rides. Watching him on the rides reminded me of the gratification he got from spinning himself on the Jolly Jumper when he was a baby, and how I had to leap across the floor every night with him in my arms just to stop him from wailing. Cade had the same focused look on his face on those rides as he did as a toddler being pushed vigorously on the swing for hours at the park. I could not wait for him to be tall enough to get on the roller coasters. I'm a roller coaster junky and would love nothing more than to have Cade and Nève share the delight I experience on those rides. James has been brave enough to come along with me a few times, but roller coasters really aren't his cup of tea.

On really busy days, we would go to the customer service counter to get a pass that would permit us to skip the lines. Generally, this pass was allotted to individuals with mental and physical disabilities, and those in wheelchairs. It meant that the individual plus up to three guests would enter a ride from the exit, show the pass, and be permitted to board immediately. If the line was short enough, we'd wait with everyone else to teach Cade how to wait for his turn. A lengthier wait would probably provoke a tantrum, so we thought we'd take advantage of the special pass for those instances. The goal for us was to achieve tantrum-free outings. We decided that we'd try to "re-circuit" Cade's brain patterns to prevent bad behavior and tantrums by going long-stretches of time without meltdowns. Cade's brain was clearly programmed to have frequent meltdowns, so we needed to replace that *data* with a new *habit* of self-regulating. We tried avoiding and redirecting his attention from scenarios that would get him worked up. Every time Cade displayed tolerance in a non-ideal situation, Sarah and I would give him abundant amounts of praise and rewards.

Some days were better than others, of course. Some days made me feel like every bit of progress we had made would be flushed down the toilet in a single instant.

There were a few episodes at the zoo and at Canada's Wonderland where Cade and I would be battling it out on the floor of a filthy, urine-soaked bathroom stall in ninety-degree heat. I can't remember the trigger for these tantrums, but I know it didn't have to make any sense or have any logical reason for occurring. They just happened... like an epileptic seizure that comes on without warning. For some unknown reason, Cade always seemed to have a tantrum in the most vile places where leaving him on the floor would simply not be an option, so the fight would be far more difficult to control.

There was one particularly intense occasion at Canada's Wonderland (similar tantrums had also been experienced at the zoo and Ontario Place). It happened in the family/wheelchair accessible bathroom in the water park section. Sarah was with us that day to look after Cade and I was taking care of Nève, though we always did everything together. When Cade needed to be dressed or had to use the toilet, I'd take over. Sarah required that I or James assisted Cade in that area which is totally understandable. While Sarah waited outside the washroom with Nève, a huge tantrum ensued. Again, I don't remember what caused it. I couldn't stop him from clamping onto the toilet seat with his jaws. His face would push up against the walls near the toilet as I fought to pull him away from the filth. The more I struggled, the harder Cade seemed to fight. I was getting scared by the seventh or eighth minute into this battle. It must have been one hundred degrees in that stuffy, wet bathroom. My sweaty hands could not manipulate Cade's slippery body for much longer. I lost my temper and began to scream at the top of my lungs at Cade,

"Stop it! Stop that!" I thought the whole park could hear Cade and me screaming. I was waiting for a knock on the door from Sarah, but she didn't knock. By now, we must have been in the bathroom for around fifteen minutes. Somehow, I finally gained control of the situation. We stumbled out of the sauna-like bathroom and noticed Sarah and Nève waiting calmly for us only about ten feet away.

"Didn't you hear us both screaming in there?" I asked exasperatedly.

"No. What happened?" Sarah seemed bewildered.

"Really? You didn't hear any of that?" I was perplexed since I thought the cops would be standing outside the bathroom door.

"No, I didn't hear a thing," Sarah insisted.

I explained the whole thing and I confessed to her that I broke the rule about showing emotion during a tantrum. Sarah's reply was along the lines of, "Oh well, what's done is done," with a tone of disappointment. That always made me feel guilty because I knew that every time I'd break in front of Cade, I'd be contributing to his developmental regressions. Still, I never felt confident that I was following Sarah's rules accurately even though I tried as best as I could. Also, I was emotionally injured and exhausted. It was really challenging for me to appear strong to Cade when I was fading by the day.

***

I remember that there were many times when I would go on brief outings alone with the kids to run an errand or something. I constantly feared dealing with one of Cade's fits. Cade's meltdowns which occurred when I left his line of sight for a second began to happen regularly and predictably. Even if I had to step out of the car, while it was still running, to throw out some trash in an outdoor bin, I'd return to a screaming, red-faced Cade who would be biting and tearing off his clothes in a fit of violence. This would then last for up to two hours. I started to become aware that this new developing problem was going to be difficult to work around and needed to be corrected immediately. Even if James was in the car or in Cade's presence and I left for a moment, it would ignite the fuse within Cade, so I knew this bad habit was based upon me alone. Before implementing the ABA strategy of leaving Cade over and over again until he became desensitized to it, I thought of trying to give him a verbal cue to let him know where I was going and for how long, in case this may have been brought on by a fear of abandonment since he was still just a toddler. I suppose I hadn't thought of doing that earlier because I didn't think Cade would understand me anyway. But I tried it. James was in the car with the kids, and before exiting, I turned to Cade and articulated slowly, "Cade, I am going to that store," while pointing to the store to make sure he understood. "I will be back in two minutes," I said while pointed to the car's digital clock. "Be a good boy for Daddy and Nève, Ok?" Cade looked at me as if all was clear in his mind. When I returned, Cade was calm and content. Of course, it was crucial that I returned within the two minutes for this to work effectively. We all cheered for Cade upon my return to reinforce this positive behavior. At later times, when I was alone with the kids and in a similar situation, I would simply have to REMEMBER to let Cade know where I was going before I would be out of sight. This small discovery made me realize that I could get much more pleasant behavior out of Cade by keeping him informed and forecasting things to come in a simple and straight-forward manner. This simplified outings for me in a significant way. Not only did it curb some of Cade's tantrums, but it served to make "normal" scenarios become more frequent. I could now give Cade easy instructions that would allow me a bit more flexibility. For example, I could instruct Cade to sit at a table in the food court of a mall with Nève while I got food from different vendors. I would tell them where I would be standing, and as long as I could see the kids and they could see me, everyone was happy, although a large part of me was quietly panicking. I would make eye contact often with Cade and wave as if to say *I see you*. Before going to the next vendor, I would drop by the table, praise the children for being well behaved and then inform them of the next place I'd be standing. Their attention was locked on me, and mine on them.

Though this was a big step forward for our family, I had no idea that my unhappiness was holding us all back.

You might wish to consider alternative therapies to complement the conventional. If you don't have the means, don't worry. It's just an aid to enhance the daily hands-on work you will do – that is more important.

I hope that recounting my experiences with Cade's tantrums will help parents with children who react violently, to understand that they are not alone. It is important to figure out what triggers the tantrums and how to prevent them. Think outside the box. Be creative in your problem-solving because the answer might not be obvious. But find comfort in the knowledge that violent behaviors do get extinguished over time if managed with strength by the parent(s).

Not all autistic children react violently. IF yours does not, consider that a blessing and a gift. If yours does, know that there is a light at the end of the tunnel, and you are not alone!

CHAPTER 8

THE TANTRUMS GOT WORSE, AND SO DID I

I used to be a bubbly, enthusiastic, and somewhat positive person before all this. I couldn't see that I was losing the part of my character that James fell in love with. Without realization, I was growing colder and angrier, to the point where I was bitchy all the time. I felt panicked and anxious all day. These feelings and thoughts fed soul-destroying misery into my family, my marriage, and me. At the time I deemed these feelings justifiable, but I've learned that nothing good ever comes from hate, anger and resentment. In hindsight, I see that James was absolutely correct with his mantra. Nothing James could say would make me feel happier. God knows he'd tried. I believe that I was clinically depressed and on a downward spiral. Despite being physically and emotionally exhausted, I was still entirely motivated to keep finding ways of helping Cade. In fact, that was my only driving force – I didn't realize that I had stopped nurturing myself and my marriage. I had become obsessed.

Recently, I was out having lunch on a Sunday with James, the kids and Sarah. We hadn't seen her in a year and every so often we like to reconnect socially. We were talking about how this book was progressing. I explained to Sarah that it was extraordinarily tough reliving all the painful moments we experienced as a family. I shared with her that during the time she was in our lives, I was really becoming mentally unstable. Cade's diagnosis had so deeply wounded me that the scars were too difficult to hide. Every time Cade displayed symptoms of autism, the wound would open again making the healing that much more difficult. I openly told Sarah that I was depressed and not myself. She totally agreed with that statement. I was surprised because I thought I was pretty good at hiding what was going on inside my head. Apparently, I wasn't good at it at all. Sarah mentioned that I was forgetful and angry all the time. James concurred. He also admitted that he had been unable to talk to me about the changes he saw in my character and behavior because he feared a terrible argument would start. James profoundly worried for me and felt helpless. I was perplexed by what I was hearing. I really had no idea that I was so transparent. Then Sarah began to reminisce about times we spent together on outings.

"You'd lost it, Tania! Remember that time Cade squirmed out of his car seat and you refused to pull over?"

I remembered that Cade had squirmed out of his car seat many times during a vicious meltdown. But I didn't recall Sarah ever being there. "No. When was that?" I answered grimacing like a fool, fascinated by the beginning of this story.

"I was in the car with you and I was screaming at you to pull over." You could see Sarah reliving that fearful moment. "Don't you remember that?"

"I honestly don't," I said. "I guess I must have blocked that out!"

James jumped in, "You blocked out a lot, hon. I don't think you remember anything! You have no idea what you were like back then." I was a little hurt and felt guilty hearing him say that. It made me recognize how much my negative thoughts had affected everyone around me.

James later described me as Dorothy from The Wizard of Oz. I was living in an alternate reality. I became blind to the world around me while living in a fantasy. Except, the fantasy that I made for myself was one of hell and hopelessness. And unlike Dorothy, I was mean – especially to myself.

"You really struggled with Cade in those days. I know you were suffering a lot and it was hard to think rationally," Sarah empathized.

"Well I'm glad I'm not that person today," I responded with my head up. "It was a very hard time for me but look at where we've ended up today." My eyes must have been beaming as I watched Cade across the table scarfing down a hamburger and some fries. He looked so beautiful to me. Knowing full well what we were discussing, both kids remained completely quiet. Nève pretended she couldn't hear anything as she focused on building her kiddy-sized tacos. Cade, sitting directly across from me, gazed up and gave me one of his looks. It's a corny smile, exaggeratedly elevated eyebrows, and gigantic doe eyes that sparkle with openness and adoration. This was followed by the words, "I love you, Mom."

***

It was around late November of 2007, Cade was four years old and his birthday was 2 months away. We moved to the thirty-fifth floor of a condo in the city. James and I came across, what we thought, was a good real estate investment opportunity. The condo building was smack-dab in the center of Toronto and totally brand new. The properties were priced to sell. You don't turn away from opportunities like that. We had plans to live there for only a couple of years and then sell it for a nice profit. I was in no mood for this! I was happy with my home and I had no energy to move and uproot our lives into the heart of the metropolitan area with two little kids. With a little convincing and persuasion from James, I actually got a bit excited about the idea of change. I imagined that I would go for wonderful walks with the kids and our mini-poodle, Charlie, along the energetic streets of the city. There would always be something to do and see. Sarah wasn't thrilled about having to drive downtown for therapy sessions with Cade. Sarah hated driving in the city but, she too, got over her initial apprehensions.

Because having less space was an issue, we converted Cade's new bedroom into a therapy space as well. We filled one wall with shelves and cube storage for all the learning materials Cade and his therapists needed. Next to the shelving unit and at the end of Cade's room, we placed a little green plastic table with two little purple plastic chairs where he and the therapists would work for a treacherous number of hours each week. It was very important to James and me to make sure Cade's room was a happy and cheery place to sleep and work. It wasn't very hard to do because at the end of the room, the entire wall was a glass window that overlooked the shiny city. So much light entered the room, it seemed impossible to ever be unhappy in there. We painted the walls sailor-blue to keep the feeling cool and calm. We placed two vibrant child-themed rugs in his room to represent separations between the work space and the sleeping space. The walls were decorated with colorful pictures and light fixtures that were shaped like the moon and stars. We hoped that Cade would be happy in that room.

Our family eventually adapted to the big change from living in the suburbs to city life. The therapists also got used to the complicated system to enter the building and the elevator ride to the thirty-fifth floor, which on a busy day, could take at least five minutes because the building only had two elevators servicing thirty-six floors. None of this was convenient for our needs at the time, but we all got used to it.

Living in the city obviously had its challenges. Lila convinced us to get a handicap parking permit because it would allow me to park in more convenient and safer places when transporting Cade. She was a practicing registered nurse before entering the field of ABA, and still had her certification. So, she signed the legal forms as our guarantor to acquire the permit. When we received it in the mail, I noticed that it would only be valid for five years. I fantasized about what Cade would be like in five years' time. I understood that five years was a substantial amount of time in a young person's life. So much could happen in that short period. That tag represented more to me than just a permit; it was more like a contract with God. If I could just stick it out for five more years, Cade would show us an incredible improvement. I felt optimistic that five years of learning and maturing would bring us to a more comfortable, easier and better place in our lives. When the permit expires, Cade would be like any average kid – I prayed for this.

In 2008, Cade had turned five-years-old. He was beginning to speak in short sentences expressing his needs and wants quite effectively. His grammar was a mess, but he was communicating and that was amazing. Therapy carried on as usual. I recall that this was an exceptionally difficult age for him though. As Cade was growing, so were his tantrums and strength. Though he was developing well as far as his cognitive abilities were concerned, Cade's behaviors were worsening. He appeared angrier with the therapists and was more defiant than ever before. Lila implemented stricter guidelines and rules in his therapy program and in our household in the hope of managing his outbursts. Nothing seemed to help. Lila removed outings from his program because she felt that his behaviors were not benefitting from them. During extra-long sessions, Cade and his therapist would be permitted to go for a walk outside for some fresh air and exercise. I was devastated for Cade that it had gotten to this point. The more he suffered, the more I suffered. Each day that passed, I would hear angry and vicious fits of destruction from behind his closed bedroom door. I would hear Cade screaming demonically and the sound of furniture being pushed and slammed. In these instances, Sarah would proclaim, "I'll just wait until you're done," which would set him off even more. I had to keep Nève away from his room during these outbursts because she was curiously hanging around while trying to understand what was going on inside her big brother's room.

"Why Cade scream?" she'd ask so innocently.

"Because he doesn't want to work and listen to Sarah," I answered simply. Nève appeared hurt and confused for her brother.

This went on for the better part of the year. It was becoming a common occurrence to have Sarah and other therapists show me damage to furniture that Cade had caused. One of the rugs had been fringed so severely at the end because Cade had bitten down on it and pulled so forcefully it tore. I am shocked that he didn't lose any teeth in the process. He would leave teeth marks along the edge of his wooden bed frame and flip the entire mattress off the bed. Sarah would come tearing out of his room, leaving Cade sprawled on the floor in hysteria, demanding packing or masking tape to tape down his mattress to the box spring. Finally, we had to tie all the drawers together to prevent potentially life-threatening injuries from happening during sessions. Cade's behaviors were getting so like that of a wild savage, everyone was at a loss for solutions.

Confusingly, but to my benefit, outings were becoming less difficult as Cade was having fewer tantrums in public. I think he'd become so exhausted from his therapy sessions that he'd be somewhat peaceful outside of therapy. Little demand or restriction was placed upon him during his downtime, so that was pleasant for him. Cade was beginning to understand that I was not going to tolerate his bad behavior for anything and I was going to be in charge of the situation at all times, not him. I would be indifferent to his protests and not give in to his irrational demands and quirks. Still, I was very apprehensive about going out to a public place with both children by myself. I feared that I wouldn't be able to keep an eye on little Nève if Cade was to have one of his meltdowns. The only time I ever went out with both kids, at this time, was when someone was with me. I'd take Nève out for some one-on-one time when Cade was in therapy or in some program, and I'd take Cade out for our special time when Nève was either out with my mom, Rowena or James. I remember taking Cade to the new supermarket in the city for the first time. I placed him in the child seat of the shopping cart as I would normally do. I'd try and turn the errand into a learning experience for Cade. We'd start in the produce section and I would hand over a fruit and ask Cade "what's this?" and "what color is it?" I'd engage with him as much as he could understand. Cade had been getting excited by all the visual stimuli that surrounded us. He was making sounds reflecting his joy. A woman on a cell phone glanced at us with a smile. I told Cade to keep down his volume a bit, but he didn't understand. Cade's noise was not inappropriately loud so I didn't push the issue. The lady continued to watch us while we strolled along the aisles. Cade continued with his happy vocal expressions. We stopped at the peaches and I grabbed a peach and gave it to Cade. He was fascinated by its fuzzy exterior and lovely fragrance. I wasn't planning to buy peaches, but I wanted to explore them with him. Cade began rubbing the peach on his cheek, so I quickly removed it from him, "No Cade, that's not clean. We need to wash it first," I explained. I placed the peach back on the stand. The woman on the cell phone ended her call abruptly and approached offensively.

"You're going to put that back with the other peaches? That touched his face!" She snarled.

"He had it to his cheek. No big deal," I responded feeling a bit confused.

"Other people are going to eat that!" she continued with a raised voice.

"I realize that," I raised my voice back, "but I generally wash the fruit before I eat it and I would hope you do too because people touch them all day long. It's not like he put it to his mouth."

"I understand but people don't like seeing that," she responded. I could not believe this woman was making such a big deal. Did we aggravate her so much that she had to cause a fuss?

"Look, ma'am, he's just a kid and I took it away from him straight away. He's autistic and I'm trying to teach him about peaches..." it felt strange but liberating to pull out the autism card.

"Oh!" she rapidly withdrew her fire, "I didn't realize..." Her tail immediately went between her legs as she backed away.

"Not everything is as it seems," I said as she walked off. I looked at Cade lovingly, "It's OK, buddy. You did nothing wrong." And we continued on with our grocery shopping adventure.

But I couldn't let go of the incident with that woman. I kept replaying it all in my mind and thinking of all the things I would rather have said to her. All the while I was playing with Cade, her words kept coming up in my head. The more I thought about her, the bitterer I became.

Both Cade and I were regressing; he with his therapy sessions, and I with my depression. I was so deeply in a state of helplessness and hopelessness that I existed just for my kids. I put on my happy *mommy face* for them. I was as loving and as nurturing as I could be. I forgot that it was equally important for me to, at least, put on a happy *wifey face* for James. Instead, I neglected him and projected onto him all of my hurt.

I hated my life. I hated autism. I hated the world in which I lived. I **hated** so much!

Sometimes, I got so caught-up in my darkness that I would fantasize about ending it all. I dreamed that it would all be easier if I jumped off the balcony with the kids from thirty-five floors high. I don't ever remember having such morbid thoughts, but apparently I did, because I wrote a personal essay about it. James found it in my night-stand and destroyed it. He described the writing as being messy and scribble-like, which is not my style. He explains that "the pain" wrote this, not me. I recollect **nothing** about this – James encouraged me to share this bit with you because we want you to truly understand that any sorrow you are experiencing is not felt alone. Remember, though, that this is a happy story!

> *The focus of treatment is always on the child. It is the child who gets the support, therapies, and extra attention. Parents of autistic children are often ignored and consequently their mental states can become harmed due to the stress. A parent's mental state must be nurtured and strengthened as well as that of the child's.*
>
> *The darker I got, the darker the violence got.*

CHAPTER 9

TIME TO FIND A SCHOOL ... AGAIN

Lila and Sarah knew that Cade's time with them would soon be ending since everyone agreed that we were at an impasse with Cade's progress. At that point, we didn't have a concrete plan on how to move forward, but it undoubtedly was time to restructure. Cade had learned an insurmountable number of practical and academic skills that he would otherwise not have learned if he'd never had ABA. Cade had also acquired the tools for self-teaching and future learning because of ABA. But, to tackle the issues of violent behavior, Cade needed a new strategy and a different learning environment.

In the summer of 2008, Sarah urged me to get Cade enrolled into school because he was now of school-age and she shared my feeling that we needed to place him among other children in a school setting.

Though I understood the importance of enrolling Cade in a school, I approached the subject with much anxiety. I couldn't face the rejections again. Which school would be best for him, but more realistically, which school would have him? Sarah said that public school was a potential option, but they were not equipped with the necessary ABA staff that Cade would require to have any chance at succeeding. Furthermore, they put all the kids with varying special needs into one classroom regardless of age. Public school was out of the question for me personally anyway. Our local elementary school repulsed me. It was the typical urban stereotypical public school that was old and rundown. Occasionally, we'd take the kids to play in the school playground which was not well maintained. It wouldn't be unusual to find a syringe lying around on the ground! Cigarette butts and marijuana roaches were commonly seen at the foot of the stairs that lead to the front doors of the school. One weekend I sneaked inside the school to have a quick look around and noticed that the walls were entirely covered in posters focusing completely on social issues like exercising tolerance of others and saving the planet. Whatever happened to the posters on the walls in the schools I attended as a child, which promoted reading, math, science and history? Isn't that what school's for? I wish the public system would get back to its roots and leave the social topics for the parents to teach.

Since twenty-five hours per week of ABA therapy was still mandatory under the contract rules with the government, we knew that this meant that every day after school and on weekends Cade would have to work with the therapists. I worried that Cade would burnout fast with this routine, but it might have been worth it if I felt that he would be getting a high-quality learning experience at public school. Since that wasn't going to be the case, it made no sense to go down that route.

Sarah recommended three different privately-run education centers that taught children with autism. One of the three schools educated students with all different developmental and physical challenges which included – but did not specialize in – autism. I wasn't totally keen to her suggestions. "I don't want Cade around other autistic kids. I want him to be around average children because he needs to be exposed to how it is to be like everybody else," I stated. "He's going to pick up all their bad habits otherwise!"

"You're right," Sarah responded. "He may be exposed to a lot of the other kids' bad habits but just know he'll have the ABA support he needs. At least go check them out."

The idea of Cade going off to school which provided ABA as the foundation of his academic learning seemed like the most sensible choice. Secretly, however, I believed that taking Cade to an institute for autistic children would solidify the fact that my child was not normal. I know that sounds horrible for me to say but understand that I was not in a healthy state of mind. And so, I was less than thrilled at the prospect of sending Cade to any autism center. But, what kind of mother would I be if I allowed my own selfish problems to get in the way of my child's best interest? What would be the harm in checking out a few schools?

Though it was summer, these learning centers were open for business. Unlike regular schools, these types of schools remain open all year long. The first school that James and I visited was in downtown Toronto. The visit was OK, but as the director of operations was giving us the tour, we noticed that most of the students were nearing or in their teenage years. One young man that we saw was being taught to shave. Cade was only five and a half, and he needed to be surrounded by children his age, so this school wouldn't make much sense. With a tuition fee of $70,000 a year per student, it was heartbreaking to see the state the school was in. (Yes, I repeat... $70,000 per year!) The director's office and the supplies room were cluttered disasters, the teaching rooms seemed filthy and desperate for a renovation, and the general atmosphere was all around gloomy and depressing. Almost all the lights were turned off which enhanced my negative perception. James and I assumed that the fees went directly to hiring teachers/therapists, which was almost incomprehensible to someone on the outside. We weren't expecting a cutting-edge facility, but the energy of that environment didn't feel right to us. Nonetheless, we put Cade on the one-year waiting list.

Later that week we visited the second school. This was our second choice because of location. It was easy to get to, and their website seemed exciting with all the programs they offered like skating and performance arts. When we got there, the place seemed quaint and warm. Each room served its separate purpose and offered brightly colored equipment for physical therapy for the students. On the tour, we noticed that most of the children were between the ages of four and fifteen years who had serious physical or mental challenges. James and I quietly gushed over the endearing smiles of these gorgeous children who greeted us. It was as if these kids could turn the world into a better place with just their smiles, even though some could not speak or walk. Though this particular school was filled with beautiful angels, it was not the right fit for ours.

We chose to see the school called Shining Through lastly because it was very out of the way, so we deemed it least likely to be our ultimate choice. It was about forty kilometers away from us, and it would take a minimum of forty-five minutes to drive there. During rush-hour, it would probably take an hour and a half. With little enthusiasm, James sneaked away from work for a bit and we made the trip there in the middle of the day. The school was an old heritage home that stood alone in a large field until not too long ago. It now shares its plot of land with a retirement home community. It was in the west toward the rural areas. On our arrival, there was a fenced playground on the property with an above ground swimming pool, monkey bars and slides. Toys were scattered along the fence on the ground. I already began to like what I saw. Inside the school, the walls were painted a playful purple and all the doors to the rooms were opened, revealing small boys ranging from five to ten years old and their therapists working at individual desks with cards and other materials. Students' drawings were up on the walls and the staff had added their personal touches with handwritten messages and notes of encouragement about the students. I felt the love and dedication of the staff unlike anywhere else before. We met with Shiri Bartman, the clinical director. She gave us a tour and explained that the house had been recently renovated. We saw toys, swinging hammocks and a treadmill at the lower level. Shiri told us that the programs were quite intense, so the students needed outlets to blow off steam. After giving her the scoop on Cade, the upsetting truth came up. "We have no available spots as of now," Shiri informed us. "It's about a one to two year waiting-list." Our disappointment was visible. "Our tuition is $60,000 a year," she continued, "but since you have funding, that can be applied toward the fee." James and I weren't as floored by the tuition price after hearing the amount at the first school. Shiri added, "It actually costs us $70,000 per student but we ask our parents to pay just the sixty. We host fundraisers to make up the remaining cost. And every year we have a gala where the parents have an opportunity to make up some of those funds for their child."

The school ran a full academic program with the same number of hours as a regular school, which is about six hours a day, so James and I would have to pay at least $10,000 per year out of our pockets. Unfortunately, in the world of autism, that's not a lot. Shiri shared with us that many of the Shining Through parents received no funding and many of them worked several jobs just to keep up. Talk about kicking them while they're down! I recognized how damn lucky we were to receive the financial assistance from the government. I pray that there's a very special place in heaven for the parents who were not as lucky. I hurt for them knowing that they have the added burden of coming up with this absurd amount of money annually, all while dealing with the pain of raising a child/children with autism. It's a real injustice.

We eagerly put Cade's name on the waiting list and went back home to our regular schedules.

Cade continued with his ABA program at home with Sarah and the other girls, but the dilemma of finding a temporary school for Cade was still up in the air. Sarah suggested the Catholic School. I was intrigued but not really on board with the idea, as usual. Cade would be forced to maintain his grueling ABA schedule outside of school hours. We were running out of options, so we had to move with a very open mind. I liked that the Catholic School curriculum would be incorporating Christian faith and morals. I liked that the word "God" would be welcomed and encouraged, not censored. Sarah said that Catholic schools have an exceptionally good reputation for their integration programs, where students with special needs participate in a regular classroom setting with an education assistant, and with a modified education plan. So, Cade would be among typical kids, have the support he needed, and have as much of a normal academic experience as possible among his peers. It was beginning to sound very palatable to me. Sarah warned, however, that these education assistants (EAs) are commonly untrained in ABA. We worried about whether the school would be prepared to deal with one of Cade's violent outbursts. Sarah said, "Tania, they can't turn him away or kick him out because of his autism. It's the law." Because Catholic schools are generally public they adhere to regulations that strongly prohibit them from not accepting admission of a student because he or she has special needs.

I called the Catholic School to schedule an appointment right away.

James and I liked the school, it seemed warm and friendly. Paintings of God, Jesus and angels decorated the hallways. Posters with statements such as *show kindness to others*, *peace and love for all*, and *Jesus loves you* were also found at every turn. The school was on summer break so there were no kids, but some office staff were there getting ready for September, which was just a few short weeks away. The man who helped us enroll Cade was named Ron. Though this wasn't the ideal time to apply for enrollment, Ron was patient, courteous, and very helpful. We explained our concerns to him regarding Cade's tantrums, asked how they would be addressed, and informed him of *how* they needed to be addressed. I kept replaying in my mind the words of Sarah telling me that it was illegal for them to decline his application. We shared with Ron how we were placing Cade here temporarily since we were waiting for an opening at Shining Through. I was very nervous but happily anxious for Cade to experience the classroom environment again, even though I felt that an ABA setting would be in his better interest at this point in his life. Ron filled out a million forms for us and made a bunch of copies of Cade's mental assessment documents, our utility bills and other papers showing proof of residence, and Cade's Baptismal certificate showing proof of our Catholic faith. Ron answered countless questions and consoled our concerns. He helped us tie all the loose ends together to get Cade registered and ready for his first day of school. Ron was very professional, and we were grateful to him for all his efforts and time.

A week before the first day of school, we got a call from Shiri at Shining Through to let us know that they had an unexpected opening. James and I were thrilled.

We contacted the Catholic School to ask if they could remove Cade from enrollment due to the unexpected situation, and to apologize abundantly. They must have hated us! Poor Ron, we'd rushed him and put him through all that trouble to get Cade into the school at the last minute. He had to arrange a school bus for Cade's transportation and he'd probably been on a desperate search for an EA with just a week or two before the start of term, which could not have been easy. I felt terrible canceling after all his efforts, but I also felt overjoyed about Cade's lucky opportunity.

The stars have always been aligned for Cade. He truly had his angels guiding the way for him because only a few days after we received the call from Shiri, we got a call from the other school with an unexpected opening again! We were so impressed with Shining Through, however, that we graciously declined the other invitation.

It seemed that the initial spate of rejection was over with and I realized that the doors kept opening for Cade. Thus far, fate had given him every prospect to succeed. Going back to the early years of his diagnosis, Cade was nearly the last to be granted public funding. He was placed with the most amazing team of therapists. He has parents and grandparents who could afford some additional treatments offered by alternative medicine. And now the schools that were hard to get into had made themselves accessible to us. Why have we been so damn fortunate? I would be lying if I said that the souls from above and God had nothing to do with this. In fact, I often joked with my mother, "Our grandparents made this happen," or "Cade's angels are really looking out for him." For James, that was the absolute truth. James privately continued to grow his spiritual consciousness without really sharing it with me. I'd made it very clear to him that I wasn't interested in growing that way with him. For me, it was voodoo, and he was nutty to be "following a path to enlightenment." I was living with far too much anger and pain to believe anything he had to say anyway. In the seclusion of his own thoughts, James would regularly speak to God and the benevolent energies surrounding him. He would ask for more opportunities for Cade, and express gratitude to God for the ones that were already given. James constantly prayed for me too. He prayed that I would find peace and happiness again. Did James' prayers help open these doors for Cade?

With the acknowledgement of all these positive prospects that had come to the forefront for Cade, I began to understand that perhaps destiny had a plan and that there was a greater purpose for all of us. Maybe Cade's purpose was to succeed and flourish as an autistic person. Everything in the universe seemed to have been aligned for that outcome to become a reality. I still wasn't totally convinced because any sense of normalcy in our day-to-day lives seemed light years away. Cade still had uncontrollable tantrums, and his learning delay was becoming more obvious as he got older. I knew there was a greater purpose for me, but it just wasn't obvious to me yet.

"Everything happens for a reason," James reminded me every time something brought me down. It also applied when something good happened too. All the hell I had gone through as a mother with regards to dealing with the diagnosis, the tantrums, being kicked out of programs and schools, the jeers from strangers, etc. have not killed me. Many, as well as myself, believe that all that had to happen to make me a stronger person. I had been given these difficult experiences for a reason and it was up to me to figure it out. Maybe it was for my own personal growth as I took so much for granted before Cade was born and I needed to be taught a life lesson. I'd like to believe, however, that it's more than that.

Be open to all types of learning institutes. Don't let titles scare you away from what is beneficial to your child. Everything in life is temporary, and you can choose a different route later.

Today, I believe all the good opportunities that came to Cade were a result of James' prayers. I don't mean church prayers, but personal requests to God (and other heavenly figures) asked with gratitude and deep belief that prayers do get answered.

CHAPTER 10

FINDING THE INVISIBLE WALL

Cade started at Shining Through Centre in early October. We had to say goodbye to Sarah and the girls after four years of near daily visits. They had definitely become part of our family. At the end of the last session, we exchanged gifts with Sarah and Lila. Sarah gave us two decorative frames on behalf of all of Cade's main therapists. In the frames were essays called *Welcome to Holland* and *Welcome to Holland part II* by Emily Perl Kingsley. Until that day, I had never heard of these stories. When I was asked to read them out loud, I sobbed like a baby. It was hard getting the words out as Sarah and Lila shared my tears. These essays are written from the perspective of a mother with a special-needs child and they are the most beautiful things I've ever read.

We felt that such a bond had been created between us and the therapy team that we promised to keep in touch from time to time. And so, we have.

It took James over an hour to get to the Shining Through Centre on the first morning commute. We'd enrolled Nève into a Montessori school about three minutes away from where James worked and where I'd started working part-time. The Centre was about thirty minutes away from there. Pretty much every weekday morning for the next two years, James would drive the kids in rush hour traffic for a total of two hours. James claimed to have mastered the virtue of patience during that period. I would pick up the kids from school when the roads were far less congested. After work, or from home, I would pick up Cade and then make my way to Nève.

Cade was really excited about his first day at Shining Through Centre. James and I had really talked it up so that he would start his first day with a positive attitude. At nine o'clock every morning, about a dozen young therapists (most fresh out of college) would flood out of the school door to greet the kids who were mostly waiting in their parents' cars. As the car doors opened, the exiting youngsters would approach the smiling staff members whose arms extended outward offering big hugs and an optimism-filled day. Some students were responsive, but many were not. It didn't matter to the animated therapists. Each child was greeted with the same genuine and joyful enthusiasm. For me, this school and the staff were not only professional, but I sensed love everywhere. The Centre was founded by parents of autistic kids who struggled to find a decent learning environment in which to place them. Shining Through was built on love. Those founding parents are such heroes to James and me for their sacrifices and vision to open this incredible establishment. It was clear that the general energy within the Centre was based entirely on love of children and love of teaching. James and I could not have been more confident and more peaceful about our decision.

The collection routine was equally as impressive. By three-thirty in the afternoon every student and their instructor exited the door two by two. The kids marched out and down the porch steps all dressed in their jackets and hats for the cooler season while the therapists were just in their indoor clothes. It was evident that the attention of the staff was on the children. The staff members were always smiling! You could hear them asking their students, "Where's Mommy?" and then replying animatedly, "Oh, there she is!"

The instructors would give a brief verbal report to the parent about their child's day. Supposedly, Cade transitioned quite well into the program. His behaviors were manageable, and he displayed some encouraging attributes. His therapist, Nitra, told me how sweet she thought he was and how energized she was to be working with him for the next few months.

I laughed when Nitra enquired, "Who is Sarah? Cade keeps calling me Sarah."

I replied, "She was his former therapist. Maybe he's just in the habit of saying her name," I was too embarrassed to tell Nitra that she had a similar visual ethnicity as Sarah, and that Cade tended to call new people by the names he already knew. He would call a new person by the name of someone else who suited a similar physical profile and/or race. For a short while, Cade would joyfully exclaim "Jeff!" (The Wiggles) every time we encountered a middle-aged Asian man and "Rowena!" when we'd find ourselves in the presence of a Filipina. I experienced a massive amount of humiliation on a daily basis. Because Cade was gaining some awareness to the physical attributes of people, he would sometimes remark on those particular features. He would start calling elderly strangers "grandma" and "grandpa" which some would find insulting while others found endearing. Cade came to work with me once and I thought I would die from embarrassment that day. One of my co-workers was a lovely young woman who was of Chinese heritage. Her face was round, and her eyes were very narrow especially when she smiled. Her name was Mindy. She was talking sweetly with Cade and he began to get very upset with her and commanded, "Open your eyes!"

I looked at Mindy and my jaw hit the floor! I was positively mortified! I fumbled around with my words trying to explain to Cade that Mindy's eyes were open – which made things worse, while I pleaded for her forgiveness. I must have sounded like a bumbling fool in panic mode. Mindy was so elegant and dignified. She laughed it off with complete kindness and grace which didn't make me feel any less awful. I think Mindy might have been laughing at me and my reaction as much as she was at Cade's statement.

Every time the kids, James and I ride an elevator with someone, we hold our breath praying that Cade will keep his observations to himself. If we notice that a stranger in close proximity has an obvious characteristic relating to size, skin color, makeup, piercings or clothing, to this day, we try to re-direct Cade's attention away because I dread having to deal with that situation again. And those situations still haunt us. Recently we ate at a restaurant, and the server had drawn thick eyebrows onto her face with makeup. James and I looked at each other and began to sweat the moment she came to introduce herself as our server. Every time Cade opened his mouth to say something, we'd jump in to interrupt. When it was his turn to order, he blurted out, "I like your eyebrows!"

I had to change the topic quickly and smoothly, "That's nice, Cade. Now tell the young lady what you'd like."

Today, Cade has gotten somewhat better at understanding that certain words and observations can hurt people's feelings. James and I never wanted to make a big deal about those things, but we continue to explain to our kids that God made people with lots of different appearances and yet we are all the same. Now Cade knows not to point out someone's obesity or old age, but with his growing awareness, he sees things in a new light that he may not have noticed before. When things are very surprising or disgusting to Cade, it's impossible to mask his reactions from strangers. One would expect it from a small child, but people are less forgiving when it comes from an eleven-year-old. Recently, James and I were really surprised when Cade said, "Oh look - family with brown skin!" when we were driving along. I could understand Cade's great interest if he had been raised in the mountains of Japan, but this is Toronto for goodness' sake! He's had classmates of all races and it was never mentioned, so we thought his reaction was strange.

Cade had me in stitches once when we were at Canada's Wonderland. He pointed at a woman wearing a burka and loudly proclaimed, "Look... a black ghost!" I walked away quickly with my head down, trying not to show my face.

A very close relative came over to spend the week with us from the US and she had developed a few skin imperfections on her neck since the last time Cade had seen her. With a look of shear repulsion, he blurted, "Eww... that's disgusting!"

I was mortified.

The person who was the object of his verbal attack is someone who loves Cade profoundly and sees him with so much compassion and understanding. That made things a teeny bit easier to swallow. Of course, he was reprimanded, and an apology was given immediately. But, Cade's focus remained on the skin imperfections which he insisted on pointing out to everyone, even after we told him to stop. Repeatedly, we commanded that he stop bringing up the topic, and explained why those types of comments can hurt feelings. Everyone was laughing, including the targeted person, but James and I tried to keep a serious face.

Generally, James and I figure that if we give little attention to his observations, no matter how embarrassing or possibly offensive, he won't feel the need to share his discoveries openly. Everything considered, I think Cade's on the right track with that, but we still have a lot of work ahead. I guess the blessing we could take from this is that Cade has gained another degree of awareness, one that is usually gained at a younger age, but I always say – better late than never.

***

By the second week at Shining Through Centre, we started hearing news of tantrums and protests in class. The therapists would never go into too much detail, but we knew that the tantrums were always tackled skillfully and with deep understanding of the ABA protocol. I completely trusted the therapists and the clinical staff who watched over them. None of his negative behaviors ever seemed more than the staff could handle. It wasn't just Cade and a therapist closed in a room anymore, they each had support within the classroom.

I think the fact that Cade was surrounded by so many young students like him influenced his behaviors positively. He saw how the other children acted, many were passive with their mannerisms, and some were explosive like Cade. Maybe he saw a reflection of himself through the behaviors of others and noticed what was acceptable and was not. After a few more weeks at the Centre, the reports of tantrums lessened drastically. Cade was thriving there as he continued to gain new skills and his behavior became well-controlled.

**

In October we finally said goodbye to Rowena as well. Both kids were at school now, and I had plenty of time to do the household stuff. She had been my right-hand woman for the greater part of the children's lives and I am deeply grateful to her for her compassionate assistance. Two years before this Rowena had gotten married to her boyfriend during one of her visits to the Philippines. After two years of fighting through red tape, Rowena's husband, Michael, became a legal resident of Canada. It was perfect timing for all of us. Rowena would begin a new life with her husband, and the Malaniaks would begin to enjoy a more regular and private life for the first time as a complete family.

I was experiencing normalcy for the first time in many years, and our home was finally private again. I was working more regularly, started exercising and had more free time to do as I pleased. I even got certified as a fitness-professional and began to teach cardio-kickboxing on some mornings and evenings. On the outside looking in, things seemed pretty wonderful for me. I still carried a ton of anger and negativity, however, which I took out on James. I nit-picked him on everything! The sadness, anger and resentment that had entered my life because of Cade's disorder, eventually became a permanent part of me. I'd allowed the disorder to consume my soul and my happiness, until there was nothing positive left. I nagged and criticized everyone and everything, and complained incessantly. I had hate-filled thoughts every second of the day, and James became my main target. I was so miserable to be around that I was pushing everyone out of my life. At this point, I had completely disconnected myself from my friends and had no social life. I faked my smiley face to my mom and dad, but they didn't buy it. Everyone was aware of my hurt but me. They even arranged an intervention! When the topic was brought up by James or my parents, I would lash out defensively. *How dare they say such things?! I'm perfectly fine.* I really believed that. Even my body was taking a beating over my mind's poisonous thoughts and depressed state. I developed a cold or bronchitis almost monthly. For a period of six months when Cade was a toddler, I got red and itchy patches on my face. It took a very insightful pharmacist, a stranger to me, to tell me that I was over-stressed and needed to work on my mental outlook in order to cure these patches. All I wanted was a cream. I also found out that I had abnormally high acid levels in my body which could've lead to cancers and other diseases. I was rushed to the hospital twice in one year to get treated for severe dehydration after going through a bout of stomach flu (or the Novo-virus). I had that stomach flu three times a year for two years! It consisted of violent vomiting and diarrhea every twenty minutes for about six hours in total. My immune system was always weak, but this was becoming a dangerously regular pattern. I ate all the healthy foods that I was supposed to. I never drank excessively or over indulged on junk foods. I took my supplements and followed all the suggestions from the naturopath. I was still very sick. My thoughts were literally poisoning my body.

I tried to hide any anger I had away from the children. I bottled my rage. The more I kept in, the bigger and darker it grew. I would smile in public to hide the truth. But if someone would cut me off on the road while driving, I'd unleash like a madwoman! You know those lunatics you see on YouTube screaming expletives out of their car windows or those people on the road who drive like demons out to kill for revenge? That was me. Thankfully, I never released this anger onto the kids. I shudder to think what could have been possible.

Though I wasn't aware of my ire, Cade was. I didn't know it then, but the more I suffered, the more he suffered.

Cade had demonstrated so much potential ever since the alternative medicine and behavioral intervention had been introduced into his daily regimen very early into his life. But, some days were so tough for him and he'd regress so dramatically some weeks. Cade's speech was coming along slowly but surely. He continued to struggle with understanding long, detailed sentences, and he was significantly delayed with his communication skills. By the age of six, Cade had progressed in so many ways, but he still had so much catching up to do. He couldn't grasp the simple concept of playing catch with a ball like other boys his age. He couldn't even understand that it was supposed to be fun. My high expectations of where I wanted him to be seemed completely unattainable. It was like we were trapped in the center of a small, foreign country where the border walls were made of invisible brick. All I had to do was find a wall and get Cade to climb over to make it to that next level. While frantically searching for that wall, I lost sight of all the beauty that was on the inside of this strange, little country. My main goal was to help Cade, and yet I never stopped to recognize and appreciate his little milestones and achievements. I was so strongly focused on getting to the end result (whatever that is), that I barely allowed myself to be present for the journey. Again, I was enveloped by only the darkness of this foreign place that I had created, and beauty did not exist there.

A massive turning point came into my life one day, so unexpectedly, which would result in a shift of energy that would affect the entire household, especially Cade.

I remember this turning point happened on a weekend afternoon in my bedroom. James and I were having one of our heart-to-heart discussions that involved some tears. He wanted to discuss how difficult it had become to live with me and my negativity, and that something needed to be done quickly or our marriage would be at a breaking point. I denied and defended myself from everything he said about me and I told him that he was being delusional. I had no awareness of the severity of my mental state or how he had been inadvertently victimized by it. James had tried repeatedly throughout the years to help me recognize this. He'd say, "It's not you that is causing these negative thoughts and feelings, it's the negative energy that's gotten into your head that's putting all this anger and sadness into you." I never understood what he meant by that and it really frustrated me how preposterous it sounded. I explained this to him and I would often put him down by saying that his voodoo beliefs were crazy. I was never going to be enlightened or happy like him, so I wanted to be left alone about the matter. This time James continued with, "This negativity is harming Cade, Tan." I finally broke down. I never felt so helpless and hopeless.

James was my rock who comforted me while I cried like a baby. We talked for an hour about all the hurt and pain I was undergoing. He was patient with me as we tried to figure out ways to help each other. James encouraged me as always to remain strong, and that he'd love and support me through this hard time and forever. He reiterated that Cade and Nève could have no better mother than me and he was truly grateful for that. We kissed and hugged while exchanging the words "I love you." James offered to do some energy work on me. I had never knowingly had James do that for me, but my mind and heart were more open to it at that moment. He asked me to lie on the bed, he knelt by my side, and manipulated the negative energy from my body and filled me with positive energy – I think. We were quiet while he did that, nothing was said, and he made no big motions or made any movement for that matter. I would compare his actions (or lack thereof) to praying.

After a few silent moments, James kissed me on the forehead and left the room to get himself some water. I hadn't felt that close to James in years. I felt lighter, like one of many large stones had been lifted from my shoulders. As James exited the bedroom, I walked to the bathroom to freshen up. As I splashed water on my face, I heard the voice in my head begin, "Who does James think he is?! He thinks he's better than me and knows more about me than I do. What an asshole!"

I lifted my head from the sink and looked at myself in the mirror like I had just witnessed a murder. I actually noticed *the voice* for the first time, "There it is!" It was truly a different entity speaking in my head that had led me to believe that I was concocting these hateful thoughts my whole life. James and many other spiritual teachers and psychiatric specialists refer to this as "the ego." For the first time in my life, I recognized that my ego had been controlling my thought processes and making them negative because my negativity fueled its survival. My lack of awareness was what it relied on to get stronger. Obviously, everyone lives with an ego, but most don't understand the harm it can cause to one's mental health, and most don't know the power it can have over one's life. The ego can be controlled by its host, but most people do not realize this, they believe it is simply who they are. This is what James was trying to tell me all these years.

I realize this sounds like science fiction, but that is not my intention. I am describing as much of my truth to you as possible. Take what you want and need from it, but, instead of discarding the rest, might I suggest that you put it away in a safe place, because you never know when you might need it...

I called for James as I ran down the hallway. He thought something terrible had happened because I began sobbing uncontrollably. I told him what had happened. He looked at me unsure of what was going on at first. I explained in more detail, and then we both laughed and cried as we embraced each other. I continued talking and James just listened with his eyes wide open. "I can't believe you knew about this and you tried to tell me..." I became breathless, but it wasn't necessary for me to finish speaking because James understood everything.

He opened the windows and sliding-doors for some fresh air.

After the dust had settled, James described to me what had happened in more detail. He metaphorically explained that he'd lit the fuse when he was working on me, and the bomb had gone off when I was in the bathroom at the sink. He could feel and see the years of pent-up darkness and filthy energy fill the whole apartment. It was like a skunk sprayed our home, and the energetic residue would linger for days. The negative energy I'd released was thick, dark, heavy and dirty – according to James' description. It was so repulsive to him that he immediately had to open the windows to release the sickness that ravaged my mind and soul for so many years.

He was relieved that his prayers were finally answered, and now our family could begin the healing process.

Every day that passed was better than the last. I began living a life where the negative thoughts I had were no longer going to rule my life. I still allowed for rational complaints and criticisms to creep into my thoughts, but the difference was that now I was aware of the negative energy in my mind and had control over it, not vice versa. I discovered a new sense of strength that came with having this control over my thoughts.

My parents finally got their little girl back. My husband finally got his best friend back.

I believe I walked right into that invisible brick wall and said, "It's about time for you and me to climb over it, Cade."

Negativity can infiltrate a parent's soul early on in their child's diagnosis and it can lead to depression. If the parent becomes aware of their vulnerability to the deep negative energy, then they will be better prepared to prevent the darkness from becoming a significant part of their lives.

With regards to the embarrassing things our autistic kids say to strangers, like with any typical child, explain and explain again the rules of social interactions. Eventually your child will understand the dos and don'ts of social etiquette. Again, don't let autism be an excuse for this habit to persist. Your child is so capable of learning – it might just take more time.

CHAPTER 11

THE IMPORTANCE OF
USING TOUGH-LOVE

Cade was turning seven. He had been at Shining Through for over a year and during that time, he had made some friends. So, we had a birthday party for Cade at Chuck E. Cheese's and invited a couple of his friends. Cade grew to love pizza to the point where it's now his favorite food. When we had gone to Chuck E. Cheese's in the past as a family, Cade hadn't shown any interest in the arcade games. The fact that playing a game skillfully earned you tickets that could be traded for prizes was irrelevant to him. The energy of the other kids is what appealed to him. So, he'd just run around the place zipping and zigzagging around the games and the patrons. When he needed a break from running, he'd go to the back of the establishment where the animatronics models of Chuck E. Cheese and his friends would do their rock music performances. There would be a camera facing the stage which you could stand in front of and other people could watch you perform on a large screen. No kids actually play with it for very long – if at all – because it was quite redundant to the average child after a few seconds. Cade would spend an unreasonably lengthy period in front of that camera if I'd let him. I often tried getting him to play the video games like the other children, but he seemed totally disinterested.

It seemed that Cade's hand-eye coordination was completely

disconnected. For example, when Cade would play a game that involved steering a car, boat or horse, he'd have no concept that turning the wheel right or left would affect the direction he would go. That was also the case for when we would go on the bumper cars at theme parks, or even riding his tricycle. We could never let Cade go on any of these types of rides alone for fear that he'd panic from being unaware that he had control of his own direction. We had tried several times to let him ride these vehicles after explaining that he controlled the direction. We'd explain in vain every time because he'd just panic in the middle of it all and scream bloody murder while all the other children watched in wonder and confusion. What seemed to occur so naturally for the other children was so foreign and incomprehensible to Cade. If Cade went on baby bumper boats or any other child operated vessel, I would always have to inform the operator of Cade's situation. I often had a very supportive response from these kind people and they'd always ensure that Cade was assisted when needed. James or I, always, had to be close at hand when Cade was on his tricycle. Not only was he riding right into curbs, but we had to stop him from scooting himself forward with his feet on the ground versus using the pedals. We constantly had to remind him about the pedals which often ended with him having a meltdown.

James was persistent with teaching Cade to ride a bicycle. He'd traded the tricycle for a bike with training wheels. James would try to get to Shining Through Centre a few minutes early every morning to teach Cade to ride in the empty parking lot. As a father who wanted nothing more for his son than to be able to play beside him, James was very motivated to teach this skill to Cade, no matter how long it would take. The teaching would stop in the heart of the winter season, but when James would re-introduce the lesson in spring, Cade was far more receptive than the time before. He had developed so much more awareness that learning became easier. Today, Cade rides a two-wheel dirt bike with no difficulty. He now understands that he's in control of his own direction – whether it be riding a bike, bumper cars or playing video games. In fact, Cade has become very good at video games. He regularly beats other kids in car races. He'd never practiced any of these types of games at home, so it seems that this skill just developed overnight with little to no prior exposure.

When entering Chuck E. Cheese's, it is policy for the patrons, to get a stamp on the hand with a coordinating number. This number is invisible unless a black light shines upon it. Before a family exits, the staff member shines the black light over the hand of the child and that of the parent to ensure the numbers match before they exit together. It's an excellent safety measure. When we arrived at Chuck E Cheese's, we got our hands stamped, and then headed over to our reserved table. Very soon after, my brother and his family arrived. We began munching on the snacks we'd ordered while waiting for Cade's friend Lucas and his family. At the entrance of the establishment we heard a small kerfuffle. Lucas and his family had arrived, but he was refusing to get his hand stamped. I approached the family to welcome them. Lucas dropped to the floor as his mom continued to hold his hand. "What happened?" I asked.

"Lucas hates getting stamped," his mother replied while rolling her eyes. I don't know what was agreed upon, but somehow Lucas was allowed in without being stamped. Perhaps the parents gave in this time purely because they didn't want to spoil Cade's party. I watched as Lucas visibly calmed down when he learned that he wouldn't have to be stamped. If the tables were turned, and Lucas was Cade, I think I'd have wrecked the birthday party. I would have made Cade have his hand stamped, and while Cade would be freaking out and making an enormous scene, I would then have to drag Cade outside until he settled down. I would then probably buy a few stamps the following day, and stamp him throughout the days to follow, expecting violent and unending meltdowns. I would do that until Cade would begin to minimize his reaction, at which point, I would reward him with an edible treat and celebratory compliments, followed by colossal applause. Being stamped would no longer be an issue for Cade in his lifetime. He would grow up going out to events without this disabling quirk. That's what I was taught and that's what I believe in. I don't think that is what parents are generally taught to do, but it is exactly what is taught at the Centre.

Cade had an extreme reaction to being photographed with the use of flash. Due to Cade's heightened senses, his eyes had difficulty acclimatizing to the brightness of the flash. He would run away from every camera he saw and yell at strangers who were taking pictures of others to stop using the flash. He would cry and fuss in every photo. His passport photo was such a disaster, we had to attach a note to the passport application explaining Cade's situation to the authorities. James and I realized that the flash might actually be painful to Cade's eyes, but we still needed to address the problem. So, we tried to teach Cade to tolerate the flash by desensitizing him to it. For a whole week James took photos of the kids constantly. He would make it fun and chase the kids around the house like he was an evil paparazzo. Cade didn't have to look directly at the camera – we were satisfied if he would just sit still and not freak out. By the end of the week, Cade would look at the camera and allow us to take a few wonderful photographs of him. Currently, Cade still doesn't like the flash, but he can tolerate it.

Many would say that Lucas' parents did the right thing by not getting him stamped. Many would argue that there's a time and a place for everything and a birthday party is not the most fitting place for ABA, or to bring-on a meltdown. Others may disagree with the tactic altogether and say that ABA is torture.

I heard about a woman whose autistic son got awards for his genius in science. She was against redirecting her son, so she would let him self-stimulate for hours and hours. She allowed him to engage in obsessive and compulsive behaviors or *stims*. I think it's wonderful and inspiring that her young son benefitted from being left to find his own way and to be true to himself so that he could receive such accolades. But I don't know what life is like for that family. I don't know whether the boy was violent or not, or whether he had play-dates or other normal interaction. I don't know this lady, her son, the depth of their story, the severity of his diagnosis or anything other than what I've just said. The truth is that autistic individuals are all different and the same approach will not work for everyone. I've tried to envision Cade in that situation. I've tried to imagine what our lives would be like today if we'd left him with no intervention. I simply cannot find any justification or reason to believe Cade would be better off without ABA or tough love. I strongly believe that in Cade's case, if we had not intervened, his neurological disorder would've taken charge of his life. He would've grown up to be destructive, harmful, reckless, dangerous, and violent towards himself and others, and he'd become depressed and feel very misunderstood in society. I think ABA helps remove the negative tendencies right out of the autistic mind and allows more room for the positive. I think living with the challenges of autism for a lifetime can be far more torturous than short-term, but intense, intervention. In Cade's situation, I know with much pain there is much more reward.

After our initial meetings with Dr. Konstance and Dr. Fabian, we learned that interrupting these mannerisms would be the key to fostering more appropriate behaviors. Cade had many odd mannerisms that needed to be stopped. One example that I've mentioned was his tendency to wave small objects in front of his eyes, toward the left side of his head. He would then follow the object with his peripheral vision before launching it across the room. He'd repeat that action until he emptied the whole box of LEGOs. We stopped that. We'd physically stop his hand in mid motion and gently force his hands into stacking the Lego blocks into a tower or some very basic structure to emulate normal activity. This is referred to as *hand-over-hand*. Cade would flip-out during the correction, but as he was very young his wrath was manageable in the security of our home.

One day, I really lost my patience with Cade's endless strange mannerisms, and I stumbled on a neat and interestingly effective trick that would not only stop the behavior but make him aware of its oddness. Cade was having one of his major outbursts and I was in no mood to address it. So out of my own frustration I began to mimic him in an exaggerated and mocking way to illustrate how annoying he was. I screamed, I bit furniture and pounded the table until my face turned red just like him. This surprised Cade. His eyes would widen, and he'd stop. Cade was completely confused by what I was doing, but eventually he would resume. He'd cry louder so I'd cry louder. He was perplexed by this but soon enough the tantrum would be over, and his attitude would shift. His eyes would show awareness and he'd smile in reaction to how silly I appeared. Ever since that moment, I have always dealt with his behavior in that way. It often distracted him from his negative actions. I truly felt like it was a very therapeutic way for **me** to cope with the stress of the situation as well. I felt that the dramatic demonstration was quite liberating. I was relieved to be able to let out some of my bottled-up garbage and at the same time teach Cade a lesson.

This method was proven to be so effective with Cade, that I began to use it more frequently for just about every unfavorable behavior and mannerism. I'd say, "Watch me, Cade," and I would perform the same crazy ritual as he did, including a demonstration of his demonic-looking eyes. Cade would be completely fixated on what I was doing. I could see him grinning with a hint of embarrassment.

Embarrassment is a GOOD emotion for an autistic person to experience since they are not commonly wired to have much or any self-awareness.

When Cade displayed this hint of a "normal" response, I'd re-emphasize my feelings with a verbal statement, "That's you, Cade. I don't like that. That's weird." We made sure that Cade understood that those types of behaviors and mannerisms were not acceptable to us and were not permitted in our presence or the presence of others. "Cade, if you need to do that go to your room. We don't want to see that."

Cade never appeared to be offended or hurt by any of those demands. In fact, I think he agreed. I believe that he always knew that my intent was never to hurt or belittle him, but to strengthen him. I wanted him to be confronted by the truth. Because of this tactic his self-awareness developed by leaps and bounds almost overnight. Cade then had the ability to identify the positive and negative behaviors of his Shining Through peers and realized that they reflected so many of his own.

ABA had been a life saver for Cade in so many ways, but I felt that this new and easy trick was an essential ingredient that enhanced the wholeness of his therapy and learning.

Today, when Cade steps out of line or begins to act up because he doesn't like something, or he's frustrated, he'll go back to old habits and begin to cry and overreact. I'll immediately join in and mimic his outburst. We are certainly a funny sight to behold. As Cade is getting older, and since it's not unusual anymore for him to see me imitating him, he gets upset with me and tells me to stop. I tell him that he's being truly ridiculous and that he needs to understand. With this new strong sense of self-awareness, he can understand questions relating to other children. "You are too old to cry like a baby. You are a big boy, so act like one. Does Nicole cry like a baby? Does Michael cry like you?" I know this comparison of behaviors resonates with him, but sometimes he just doesn't want to give me the satisfaction.

"I want to be a baby! I don't want to be a big boy!"

After I tell him to take a few deep breaths I demand that he calm down. If Cade continues to wail or talk back to me, I'll threaten, "If you don't stop crying right now, I will take away your iPad for the whole day!" That works every time! We used to put him on the *thinking bench* or in *timeout* before he had any interest in iPads.

Cade hates being punished, and it really hurts him to know that his behaviors and bad attitudes disappoint us. He's so sensitive that he can actually *feel* us. That's one of the millions of things we love most about him!

I made very special friendships with other parents of autistic kids throughout our journey. We became friendly with one father in particular, Roger, and his son Hector. Hector was a very bright boy who was significantly more verbal than Cade, and who established eye-contact with others reasonably well. Hector seemed very receptive to outside information and had so much potential for learning and mastering social etiquette and learning self-awareness. Hector was obsessed with fireplaces, he knew all there was to know about every fireplace that was ever made. He could spot them from miles away, and then would disrupt any conversation by purging all the knowledge he had about that specific fireplace. Hector would flicker a gas fireplace on and off at a person's house to watch it ignite and extinguish. Hector would also rock back and forth compulsively, and repeatedly bring up topics of conversations that finished minutes or hours prior. He would interrupt our conversation by asking the same question he had only asked moments earlier and repeat that question throughout the visit. Hector would ask me a question several times like, "Tania, how old are you?" I would reply, "I already told you, Hector. Do you remember the answer?" All the while, Roger would just accept the situation unresponsively. Maybe he would laugh it off, shrug his shoulders, or just repeat what I had said with no conviction.

There have been many instances where Cade would repeat himself compulsively, but our chosen reactions were very different.

We would tell Cade that he'd already asked the question, or made the statement, and we would reiterate our response. If Cade repeated himself again, we would provide an ultimatum, "Cade, you already asked that, and we already gave you an answer. If you ask again, we will take your iPad (or other item) away for the whole day." That was very effective in ceasing the repetition. But sometimes he would err, and we would have to follow through with the consequence. Because Cade was made aware of the potential consequence, he'd put up little to no fight when the punishment was handed out. "If you ask again, we'll take your iPad away tomorrow as well," we would warn. Cade would often get teary-eyed, but we understood that the key to changing his behavior was to provide consistency and follow through with a consequence to his defiance. James and I have used this strategy many times, and today, Cade rarely repeats out of compulsion.

When Roger's family and mine went out to dinner or on an outing, I noticed how the things that would bother me did not bother him or his wife. Hector rocked back and forth – I would not have tolerated that from Cade. When Cade began rocking as a toddler and when he walked from wall to wall in the corner, it concerned me. I didn't like how it could draw negative attention to him in public. So, James and I worked with Cade to stop these mannerisms before they could turn into an obsessive pattern. Like the way he was stimming with the LEGOs, we simply did not allow him to carry on that way. We would re-direct his attention to something pleasant and distracting, like a toy or puppet. Cade would stop what he was doing and walk towards the puppet with delight. Or James would scoop Cade up into his arms, throw him onto his shoulders, and trot around the house in a fun way. Because the obsession was just beginning to develop, intervention was easy, and the habit was easily breakable. We must have had the ABA instinct in our blood.

I can't say for sure whether Hector's rocking bothered his

parents or not or whether they had attempted to stop the problem, but just like with a typical kid, in my experience, all behaviors and habits can be adjusted according to the child's needs, abilities and understanding. I remember how tough it was to break Nève's habit of sucking her thumb. We used the same tactics on her, as we would with Cade. We treat Cade the same as we treat Nève. We do not excuse Cade's compulsive activities because he is autistic. In fact, we find that autism gives us a greater reason to intercept these behaviors whenever they are apparent. We understand that often with autism, behaviors, habits and compulsions get worse and are harder to change if they are not addressed immediately and constantly. Because we addressed Cade's behaviors, we now do not experience tantrums in public places anymore. Some habits can take years to break, but if the determination is there, it is possible to end the undesirable behavior.

Sometimes parents can completely lose their motivation to re-direct and correct behaviors on a constant basis. It is physically and emotionally exhausting and punishing to the parent, and progress can be so slow that we can easily become discouraged and give up. I would be totally drained when arriving home from a family outing where every occasion was an intense and physical teaching experience. I understand how easy it would be for a parent to just stop fighting against a continuous barrage of autistic behaviors and decide that it's just so much easier to co-exist with them instead. That lackadaisical attitude, however, is harmful to the child's future and the future of the family.

Sometimes strangers would notice Hector's habitual rocking and realize he was autistic. Often they would send a smile of support and understanding to him and his family or even approach Hector's family to offer some anecdotal story of their own personal experience with autism. Cade on the other hand wasn't given a second look, which is entirely the opposite to our old experiences of public meltdowns. I feel greatly rewarded by that. I say this to exemplify the polarity between two autistic boys with slightly varying degrees of autism (Cade being the weaker), and how continuous intervention can seriously affect the outcome of that child's lifelong behaviors and tolerance levels.

Over the course of time, James and I have learned that autistic children can be taught to do the simple things that typical people do naturally, such as establishing eye-contact with others, laughing at jokes, engaging in social pleasantries, and expressing affection. One of Cade's first learned skills was eye-contact. Sarah would shield Cade's peripheral vision with her hands by cupping them at both sides of his face. She would get up close to him and stare into his eyes. Whenever he looked at her eyes, no matter how briefly, she would reward him with a cereal morsel and copious amounts of praise. The ritual continued until longer stretches of time were spent looking into her eyes. Today, nearly a decade later, Cade continues to implement this skill in everyday life and I am confident that it now happens naturally.

There are four main tools I've utilized to stop annoying behaviors, with good results. They might all work together or one may work better than the others depending on the circumstance:

Desensitization *is when you bombard your child with whatever they cannot tolerate until complete acceptance is achieved.*

Re-direction *is the transferring of focus from an unwanted mannerism to a more suitable action or activity.*

Hand-over-hand *is used when your child is playing with an object or toy inappropriately, and you then manipulate your child's hands to begin playing or acting appropriately with the toy or object.*

Imitation *is my favorite because I find it is therapeutic for me but also achieves a great response from Cade. Real self-awareness comes with this method. Follow imitation with verbal explanations that emphasize your disapproval of the strange and unfitting conduct.*

Give your child extra time to gain the skills that most kids acquire early in life with no effort. Your child is different, but still very capable! Autistic children develop unconventionally. Do not stress over these things but continue to teach them the skills you want them to learn. If you feel like a break is needed, try re-introducing the learning process a few months later – you may see an enormous increase in your child's reception and learning the second time around. The point is, don't feel discouraged when your child shows no normal activity in playful settings. Teach them what's right and "normal" and understand that improvement will come later... but don't stop teaching.

CHAPTER 12

NOW, HERE'S THE
REAL MEDICINE!

Ever since I experienced my own version of enlightenment, things began changing for the better. I began to appreciate what was extraordinary about Cade and what made him so unique. I stopped judging him for what was wrong. I began to embrace and champion all that was right and wonderful about him. I no longer compared him to other children his age. I began to challenge him based on his own prior achievements. I celebrate every one of his successes as if we'd won the lottery, and in return, Cade rewarded us with more success.

The more I surrendered to God, the more I found peace. The more gratitude I gave to God, the more gifts I received. I now realize with every ounce of my being that God had a plan for me, as Cade's mother. I have learned so much about my own abilities and strengths. I feel stronger than ever and more positive and appreciative for all the miraculous things that have happened to our family that I would otherwise not be able to recognize if Cade hadn't entered our lives.

Cade had an extreme improvement by around the age of seven or eight. His communication skills had improved very significantly as he began to form longer, more complex sentences, and began sharing more of his ideas and opinions rather than just stating facts. Cade's understanding of what others were saying had also developed a lot.

I don't believe that my new-found joy and happiness, or my new outlook on life was influencing my perception, because I know that Cade's changes were entirely due to my energy shift. I credit everything we've done thus far to his growth: the alternative medicines, the therapies, and the therapists. But I think the most valuable remedy a mother can give her beautiful, sensitive, autistic baby is her own inner peace.

Let's put it this way. We all know the saying "healthy moms make healthy babies." That's logical and sensible, right? Energetically speaking, notice how hyper moms make hyper babies and calm moms make calm babies generally. The baby comes from the mother, so it's very understandable that the baby will carry a lot of the mom's energy, feelings, and emotions. The baby will know his or her mother by her smell and energy for the first weeks of life outside the womb. The mother will know when her baby is hungry because her breasts will engorge and leak. The baby and mom are totally in sync with each other. I now believe this is the reason both Cade (especially) and Nève were loud and fussy babies. Long before Cade's diagnosis and long before my pregnancies, I carried a lot of negativity around that I'd manufactured in my mind. I allowed a lot of things and people to really annoy and anger me which I would think about all day long to the point where those thoughts would become poison in my body. This poisonous energy attaches to the baby in the womb so when the baby is born, he or she will likely reflect the behaviors of the mother's general energy. Both Cade and Nève were screamers. Nève began to settle at about three months of age but was still very easily agitated. And Cade was significantly more unsettled up until about six months of age.

If you have an autistic child, you may very likely agree that he or she is extremely sensitive. They display unusual or exaggerated reactions to light, sound, texture, etc. Now, let's imagine a baby was born highly sensitive to the point where they have an extra acute sixth sense. They can feel all the surrounding energy, good and bad. With autistic babies, I think the level of energetic connection to the mother is off the charts. So much so that if a mother is unstable, unhappy, mentally imbalanced, depressed, negative or generally angry, then the autistic baby will feel all of it. That baby will react to the general energy that the mother carries. When the mother suffers, the autistic baby suffers.

The amazing thing about autistic babies is that they do not separate energetically from their moms as they get older like do typical babies. When a mother discovers that her child is autistic, or she suspects something is wrong, this feeling of suffering and hurt only heightens the symptoms of autism in the child. If a mother is blessed enough to find peace under these circumstances, the child has a much broader chance of succeeding with the help of intervention and other therapies. As long as a mother carries the burden of pain and unhappiness about her child's state, it doesn't matter whether she provides him or her every therapy under the sun – therapy will not work wholly or at all until the mother is in a healthy state. Her mind must be cleared from negative thoughts and her heart must be open and at peace. How does one tell a mother not to freak out about an autism diagnosis?! It's not possible for a loving parent to react any other way when faced with such difficult or unexpected news. I get it!

Let it all out of your system now. Whether your child was diagnosed yesterday or twenty years ago, get rid of that pain however you can. Talk about your feelings with loved ones, see a professional, or meditate. I find writing very therapeutic. Cry it all out then cry some more. If you haven't grieved enough because you felt that you had to be strong, let it out now. Dump all that negative garbage out of your system. It may take one good cry, or it may take a series of them over the course of weeks or months. Purge all the negativity associated with the pain of having an autistic child. I also strongly suggest that you stop thinking about what caused the autism. Reliving the moments and situations of the past that you suspect caused your child's autism does absolutely nothing to help your child. In fact, it brings the negative energy into your life which then harms your precious child. You must start a new day with the belief that God chose YOU to take on this life challenge and there was NOTHING you could have ever done to prevent this outcome. *This lesson was made for you with the most **loving** intention.*

It is your choice how to move forward: you can let autism defeat you and paralyze you with sorrow and regret, which will certainly cause your child to regress, your health to be compromised, and your marriage to fail. Or you can understand as early as possible that this is a blessed life lesson that will ultimately teach you the most amazing things about yourself. It can enrich and enhance your life and who you are as a human being. It can strengthen and unite your family, not tear it apart. You can gain a huge sense of fulfillment, and admiration from others, not pity. Maybe these and other written words of hope are enough to infiltrate your life so that you can find the peace and happiness that is required to get you and your child on a path to healing. Make sure all that trash is gone for good, and that will be the last time you will ever feel sorry for yourself and your child.

If you did not give birth to your child, the same rules apply. Your child lives with you and by now has established an unbreakable bond. They *feel* you as well as everyone else in their vicinity. Why do you think crowded areas are so hard for them? Autistic children pick up on all the energy around them – they are sensitive to each individual on their own and collectively as a group. Some people are good, and some are very bad and the mix of energies can be an overwhelming sensation for autistic children.

Your home needs to be a sanctuary. Actually, this advice would serve all parents. When I refer to the term sanctuary, I don't mean that your home needs to be filled with luxuries, new furniture, and kept clean and tidy all the time. But the energy of the people in the house has to be harmonious. Mom and Dad mustn't fight in front of the kids, better still, they must be happy with one another. If parents carry deep seeded animosity or any kind of hatred or intense displeasure towards their spouse or partner, the child will feel that negativity and likely delve deeper into their invisible cocoon that is autism. Arguing with each other, especially in front of the child, may cause your child to regress developmentally, and may interfere with their possibility of making gains. Name calling and bad language must stop. When things get testy, as they do in any normal household, take a deep breath. Exhale the negative feelings, anxiety, frustration or whatever, and then talk about it calmly. If you don't, it will fester in your mind, morph into your environment, and become that negative energy that harms your child. Resolve issues as soon as possible.

Parents of autistic children must unite as a team as much as possible. They must be supportive of each other. If the two parents are able to unite fully with the intent to address the challenges ahead together immediately, it makes for a better child, a better home, and a better marriage. The lines of communication must be wide open and loving. Nagging must end and communication must begin. Show the affection you have for each other to your children. Also, be physically affectionate toward your children equally, but exaggerate this for your autistic child. Some examples include – but are not limited to – kissing, hugging, caressing, tickling, and playful wrestling. The more you lovingly and joyfully touch your child, the more you will break through into their world. You will begin to desensitize them from the negative reaction they experience from physical contact.

The divorce rate among parents with autistic children is a staggering 85%. I think the main reason for this is because one parent cannot face the reality of their child's diagnosis, and remains in a state of denial, while the other parent strongly believes in the diagnosis and fights to get the other to get on board so that they can work together as a team. Also, it's common for one parent to become depressed and withdrawn because of their grief, leaving the other parent feeling lonely and emotionally abandoned. The painful feelings associated with learning the news of your child's "disability" may manifest differently in each parent, which then causes conflict, feelings of distance and alienation from each other. The heightened level of sorrow and darkness that can engulf the home of an autistic child can be the most toxic and harmful place in the world. Under those circumstances, one can understand why a child would not want to peek out of their isolated and self-made invisible cocoon. It would be far too agonizing, to put it mildly. Parents need to fix themselves first! Seek professional help if necessary.

A new friend of mine, whose son had recently received the diagnosis at the age of four, had shared with me that her marriage had been suffering. Her husband was having trouble accepting the news of his son's diagnosis and she felt that he was pulling away from the family unit. I recommended that she should stop using the term "autism" in their house or when referring to their son. I prefer her to approach her husband lovingly and supportively with this sentiment:

"Our son is perfect how he was created. He just needs some help with getting on track. I will do everything in my power to guide him and help him as much as possible. I need you to be my teammate. We chose each other for this life's journey, and our son deserves us to honor that decision. I love you and I want to address this challenge alongside you. If this is how we vow to go forward, our son will have the best chance of succeeding, and we could all find joy in the process as a family."

It's very therapeutic to know that your partner in life is sharing your feelings, and you are not alone. You both have your child's best interest at heart, so work together, not apart. But be sure to not let the marriage be all about the child! Go out on dates... lots of dates.

Ideally, once a week. It doesn't have to cost much either. Go out for coffee or tea. Talk about things other than your child or children. Reminisce about what made you fall in love. Be sexy for your spouse. Dress up once in a while. Go get drunk together or whatever floats your boat. The point is that you need to keep the harmony in your marriage. Remember that FEELINGS of LOVE are a massive component in treating autism. It's all about energy, energy, energy!

I don't want to mislead anyone by suggesting that our home is perfect. We're human too in the Malaniak household. We've had our struggles along the way as I've already explained. But, I can say without a doubt that our home, in general, is now a warm and healing place for our children to thrive. If you can say that, then you're on the right track. If not, it needs to be corrected as soon as possible for the sake of your child's chances. I've offered my experiences, both good and bad, as guidelines for having a strong head-start in improving the lives of our phenomenal autistic children and, consequently, our own.

In some cases the only way to create a sanctuary-type atmosphere at home is for the parents to separate. Raising an autistic child in a happy two parent home is tough, so doing it alone must have significant challenges, but all I can suggest is that you surround yourself with loving friends and family to give you the strength and support when you need it. Take time for yourself and re-charge when you can. Take time to enjoy life and do the things you love to do. There's no real point in trying to help your kid if you're emotionally imbalanced and/or your marriage is unhappy. Clean up your own life. Find joy. We all deserve that.

After some months passed, I began to watch the interactions between the parents and students of Shining Through more intensely to see how my theory applied to the development of the other students. I saw deeply rooted emotional pain in the faces of most of the parents as well as an extraordinary amount of love. I saw my former self reflected in these parents. I wanted to scream out, "It's all going to be OK!" I would see these exhausted moms and dads waiting to reconnect with their children only to receive no reaction. I would see the blank looks on the students' faces and the defeat in the eyes of the parents. In conversations with them in the parking lot, I would point out some noticeable potential I'd see in their child as a supportive and sincere gesture. My opinion would not have been met with much agreement, acceptance, or optimism in many cases, and then, the topic of autism would likely be brought to the forefront of the discussion. Newly tried oils, diets, naturopathic methods and every other form of treatment were shared among the parents, none of which made much of an impact. I wanted to tell them about the great strides Cade had made and how we were moving forward with such velocity, but I was hesitant to do so. I didn't want to come off as gloating or smug since Cade's progress compared to many of the other students was obvious.

I knew in my heart that I would be viewed as a wacko if I told anyone that their child's healing would need to start with their own healing. I mean, how absurd does that sound? I can't say that I'd blame them. And who am I to give any advice? I'm not a professional! How would I be received if I'd said, "All the therapy your kid gets at the Centre isn't enough by itself – you need to work on your energy as well."

After my own awakening, my sixth sense opened up a lot. I was able to feel the mood of others more clearly than before. I was able to feel the utter sadness emanating from many of the parents. Again, it was so familiar to me. Many, like me, smiled and joked around with the other parents, which seemed very healthy. But the soul beneath the skin was raw from injury. I felt the suffering that occurred within them and I knew that for many, home was a place of little peace. It killed me to understand their suffering and not be able to do anything to help.

I was also struck to learn that in many cases, the Shining

Through parents were not applying ABA strategies at home. I understood that the learning for many of these students stopped at three-thirty at the Centre. I began to realize with more certainty that they simply didn't know how imperative it was to apply ABA outside of school and at all times. Did the therapist's advice fall on deaf ears? Were the parents just too drained to put in the endless effort? Or maybe they weren't even told at all! I believe that most parents weren't made aware that the most critical part of their children's education was at home. How could they know? It was a gift to have had Sarah at our house with Cade. Not many parents were afforded that experience. I learned her techniques during those twenty-five hours per week in our house. She donated at least an hour of her own time, on countless occasions, teaching me the true essence of what it is to be an ABA parent. Most of these parents never had that sort of opportunity. Courses were occasionally offered to parents through the Centre from outside sources, but they cost money and took up large amounts of time, which these parents already lacked.

Many students had been brought to the Centre from the time they were diagnosed as little tots, hoping that the therapists alone would help to improve their situation. I have come to realize with so much clarity that educating the parent of an autistic child is equally as important – if not more so – to get the most palpable results from the child. I know that these incredibly loving and heroic parents would travel the world if they could find answers for their children. Many work two or three jobs just to keep their kids at the Centre. The immense financial burden on these families is incredibly difficult. There is no denying that they would do everything and anything possible for the children they adore. I see their desperation and remember it well. I also know that the love they have for their precious children is godly.

My great desire is to spread the abundant amount of hope that I have for all of God's autistic children and families. I am deeply sympathetic to the parents who have also been swallowed profoundly by the darkness in which I once lived. I know it seems overwhelming, but escaping the darkness will end the stagnancy of their children's progress.

I want to share my wisdom learned through experience, and gifted to me from the Man Upstairs:

- ***Enroll in a course to learn ABA/IBI, or read about it and apply it.*** ABA must be a new part of your family's lifestyle. When it becomes implemented regularly, it will be required less as time goes on.

- ***Make peace with autism.*** Your child is awesome! Love everything about your child because he or she is created perfectly. Many beautiful lessons will be learned in this life's journey.

- ***Find peace within yourself, and within the family unit.*** An environment filled with joy and happiness is welcoming to any child, especially an autistic one, so create this sanctuary-atmosphere in your home and watch your child break out of his *autism cocoon.*

Take time to finish the grieving process as thoroughly and as soon as possible. Release any leftover sadness and baggage you carry over your child's diagnosis. After the grieving is over, you will face each day with pride, admiration and encouragement for your child, and this will bring you peace and healing to your child. This has healed Cade, and continues to do so. Do not put too much focus on what your child can't do. If it is important and needs to be tackled embrace it; let it go when it doesn't serve you.

*A healthy and stable marriage is very important when raising an autistic child. If you are going to start anywhere on this journey of healing please consider beginning with the healing of your marriage. Like a snowball effect, this improvement will change the general energy of the house, which is good for **everyone**.*

If you are single or you are in a marriage that already has a solid foundation, start finding peace and joy for yourself. Surround yourself with people who make you happy. Read books, watch movies, and listen to uplifting music throughout the day, whenever possible, to fill you up with joy and positivity. I blast Disney music throughout the house and the kids and I, and even James, love how it makes us feel.

If your marriage has resulted in divorce or you are going through one, release all negative attachments and thoughts you have over your former spouse. Have respect and kindness for one another if only for the sake of your child(ren).

CHAPTER 13

SO MANY NEW TRANSITIONS

Not a single day goes by where we don't express our profound love, admiration and pride for both our kids. Every day, to this day, James and I tell Cade how smart and brilliant we think he is. And they are not simply manufactured words that we feel we are obligated to say as his parents, they are genuinely felt from the bottom of our hearts, and most importantly, Cade *feels* it. The more James, the family, and I focus on Cade's intellectual triumphs with true emotion and sincerity, the more intellectual brilliance he gives us. When I praise Cade for how well he uttered a sentence, he continues to challenge himself verbally, thus often surprising us with new vocabulary and detailed phrases. Cade still has a long way to go, but progress is steady and his personal desire to learn and improve is present – what more could I possibly expect from him?! I know his potential is grand, and I have real faith that his communication struggles will become fewer and fewer as he grows into adolescence.

There are times in the day when Cade's auditory mechanisms get really lazy. For instance, after a long day at school, Cade's ability to comprehend and respond to the conversations at the dinner table diminishes significantly. It is such an exhaustive task for him to process verbal information and then respond to it all day long, that he just gets tired of trying at the end of the day. Though it's totally understandable, we still don't allow Cade to shut down when we are having family discussions, no matter how frivolous they are. Sometimes, he'll totally ignore us while in a deep state of daydreaming, but we raise our voices and insist that he replies to our questions or comments. Cade usually lets us know how displeased he is to have to engage with us, but too bad – he can't get into the habit of ignoring people because it's too much work to listen. Again, we will never permit autism to interfere with normal behaviors and expectations. The moment that loved ones accept that the autistic person must be treated with modified social expectations is the moment that they stop evolving.

In fall of 2010, we sold our condo in Toronto. Cade was seven years old and soon approaching eight. We had been living in the city for about three years and had had enough of the metropolitan urban life. The commute to and from schools and work was getting more tiresome with all the increased traffic. We longed for more tranquility, and a more family oriented place to raise the kids. James and I dreamed of having a yard again, and living in a community filled with young families where it would be usual to see kids riding bikes, people walking their dogs, and neighbors stopping to say hello. This would be our chance to move closer to work and closer to the kids' schools.

Cade was doing incredibly well at Shining Through. The therapists continued to express excellent feedback about Cade's progress and skills development. His ability to learn and master new concepts was at an all-time high even to the point where they were beginning to consider placing him in a mainstream school. This was music to our ears, and it confirmed the importance of a positive mindset.

Shortly thereafter, we received notice from the government that Cade would soon be dropped from the funding program. Our funding would finish at the end of the school year. The timing could not have been more fortuitous. Cade was ready to move on and the whole universe was cheering him forward.

***

We found a home north of Toronto in the suburbs. This house needed some renovation. The skeleton of the house was strong and healthy, but the style was not right for us. The backyard, however, was the biggest in the area. It backed onto a ravine, and on the opposite side of the ravine was a church that sounded its bells three times a day. Locally are five schools and three major grocery stores in walking distance. There were cafes, shops, and just about everything you could ever need or want in a neighborhood. Canada's Wonderland was a five-minute drive away and one of Ontario's largest and newest malls was about seven minutes away. Yet, you could still brush the squirrels off your car's windshield every morning, and the sound of children playing outside is never very far away. Furthermore, we scored a house in a cul-de-sac where there was no unnecessary traffic. We found a gem and could not wait to get the renovations started.

Now we were faced with the familiar task of finding schools for the kids. Cade, of course, was the real challenge. Though there were more than enough schools in our area, James and I had our hearts set on Montessori for both kids. The classrooms are smaller and the teaching style is very hands-on. The Montessori philosophy is to teach based on the child's individual needs. Seems ideal for Cade, right? Maria Montessori started her methods of teaching primarily for those who had learning delays and challenges. It was found to be so successful that it became available to all children. So naturally, as far as mainstream education is concerned, Montessori was by far the most logical choice for Cade. We must have visited and contacted four schools in our area. Either they were completely full, or they only had the Casa program, which meant that they did not enroll students older than five or six. The one which James and I had our eyes on was not able to accommodate Cade with his special requirements. They already had two special needs students in each class and they didn't have the resources to take on another special needs student. Cade was becoming so independent that I argued that he would not be a strain on the existing structure. The school director empathized with us and offered to meet with Cade and someone from Shining Through who had recently worked with him. He would also be asked to do some of the worksheets they were teaching in class to see if he was able to do the work independently and well enough without any special help. Only then would the director consider adding him to the group.

After two one-hour encounters over two consecutive days, the director invited James and I into her office for the outcome. I was so nervous! I so desperately wanted Cade to be accepted into this school, it was made for him. The school was clean, fresh and had a new feeling to it. The walls were covered in art done by the students, and the children seemed so peaceful and content while they worked in their organized little classrooms. The student numbers appeared intimate, not sparse. The atmosphere was homey and welcoming; I knew Cade would be so happy there. The likeliness of this not working to our advantage had really been weighing on me. Our options were limited otherwise. This had to happen!

While sitting in front of the director's desk, James could see I was anxious. He loved this school as much as I and we sat holding our breath. The director began to talk about how smart and cute Cade was, and how much she would love to have the resources to accommodate him, but she had determined that though Cade was clearly showing many signs of independence and potential for learning, she felt that he would still require extra attention, which the school could not provide at that time. Disappointment was not the word to describe how I felt; it was much more painful than that. I could not stop myself from shedding tears right there and then. James explained to her about the countless rejections we had faced over the years. Maybe this one stung the most because Cade had come so far with his behavioral and cognitive changes that it was like we were being castigated for having real hope. The director, however, was very heartfelt in her response to my emotional display by offering some sympathetic and encouraging words. James and I left the school humbly. I called my mom when we got to the car because she was waiting for the verdict in anticipation. James had to take the phone from me because I was unable to speak while trying to hold back my tears. He said with my mom's agreement, "everything happens for a reason." I just rolled my eyes as I always have. Frankly, his clichés were getting on my nerves!

I rebutted, "This was the perfect place for him, James. Where do we go from here?"

"I know you're frustrated and disappointed... I am too!" he added, "but getting upset isn't going to help the situation. That Montessori wasn't the perfect place for Cade because if it was, we'd be enrolling him now. There's a perfect place for him and we'll keep looking."

I considered home schooling, but Cade needed the daily presence of children his age with whom he could interact, socialize and play in order for him to continue flourishing. Honestly, it would be much more comfortable for him to just stay home alone with me, but Cade's comfort level was not my concern. I could just envision him regressing with every passing week under those circumstances.

When we moved to this new area we ended up about three minutes away from Rose, my work colleague and friend. She had two children, so naturally I decided to ask her about her children's school. They both went to Blessed Trinity Catholic Elementary School and seemed to have been having a good experience there. Rose described the curriculum to the best of her ability. She told me that as well as French, they taught Italian too. Our neighborhood was densely populated with Italian-Canadians; in early fall, you could still find many households making jars of homemade tomato sauce in their garages. It fondly reminded me of my grandparents who'd lived in Montreal. Learning French in school is mandatory in Canada, but learning French or Italian was not beneficial to Cade at that time. We hoped Cade would focus on getting English right first before adding to the confusion by learning different languages. The languages program, however, would be beneficial for Nève. She only had one more year at her Montessori school after this one. Rose had some very nice things to say about many of the teachers who had taught her kids. She highlighted the fact that most of the neighborhood children go to Blessed Trinity. That detail was very appealing to us. She thought it would be in my interest to arrange for a visit. In Canada, elementary schools run from Junior Kindergarten to Grade 8. We learned that Cade would be placed in Grade 2 when it was time.

It was about November when James and I arranged for a meeting with the principal at Blessed Trinity, Ms. Kwiatkowski. She had a very kind and gentle demeanor. She was the soft-spoken type you'd only see in children's movies. James and I talked about Cade and his needs. Ms. Kwiatkowski gave us a tour of the school and answered all of our questions with compassion and optimism. She explained that there were already a number of children with special needs at Blessed Trinity. They participated in regular classrooms with regular kids, and they received all the necessary support systems to have a successful academic experience. This was what I needed to hear. Ms. Kwiatkowski made it clear, however, that ABA was not yet practiced by the education assistants who would likely be working with Cade. We were pleased, anyway, that Ms. Kwiatkowski had agreed to allow a therapist from Shining Through to come to the school to help Cade and his EA with the transition and to give advice.

Ms. Kwiatkowski told us that one of her Grade 2 teachers had a son who went to Shining Through. If that wasn't a clear sign from heaven, then I don't know what is! Ms. Kwiatkowski informed us that every Friday they had a pizza lunch, and Cade was thrilled about this since pizza was his absolute favorite at that age. THIS seemed to be the perfect place for Cade! Was James right again? Everything happens for a reason?

James and I were so impressed by what we'd experienced during our visit to Blessed Trinity. Again, the school hallways were filled with murals of Jesus and Mother Mary. Colorful pictures, art work and crafts decorated the walls. The school was at the center of our wholesome community, and it felt safe and right. I felt a strong parental presence in this school, like the teachers were moms and dads and the general staff cared about the students on a personal level. Though Blessed Trinity had almost seven hundred students, it seemed as though the school was much smaller than that.

There was a consensus among all of us that Cade's first experience at Blessed Trinity should be alongside a familiar ABA therapist to help him get into the new routine of his new school as smoothly as possible. Shining Through chose Nicole to take on that responsibility. She was a friendly young therapist who we had gotten to know very well over the last few months. After Nicole had filled out and submitted the necessary documents and had had a thorough criminal record check, it would take an astounding five months to receive approval from the government to permit her to enter a public school classroom for a week. Cade's first day at Blessed Trinity was in April. Cade would now be eight years old. As the old adage goes, *good things come to those who wait.* Everyone was eagerly awaiting this moment, especially me.

Cade's first day at Blessed Trinity went very well. He seemed excited to encounter so many new youngsters his age. The real gift in all of this was that his teacher, Mrs. Girardi, was the mom whose son was a student at Shining Through. In fact, Mrs. Girardi was one of the founding parents. In James' and my mind, there was no bigger sign of affirmation from God than that, and no better scenario for Cade to move into the mainstream system than under this circumstance. James was right, indeed – everything truly does happen for a reason. No other teacher in that school had as much knowledge and understanding of Cade's challenges than Mrs. Girardi. James and I actually knew Mrs. Girardi not by name but by face only because we had met her very briefly during the yearly Shining Through gala fundraisers. So when we saw her for the first time at Blessed Trinity, we recognized her instantly. We embraced like old friends. She explained how thrilled she was to have Cade in her class and how her students were so eager to have him join them. Mrs. Girardi conveyed to us that she had explained Cade's background to her students, and she'd allowed them the chance to ask questions before he arrived. According to Mrs. Girardi, the students had asked anxiously every day when they would finally meet their new classmate. Supposedly, the anticipation was enormous. Now that he had finally joined the group, the children had completely accepted him with open arms and hearts. Actually, the only trouble was that the students would have to *share* him! Over the first week, Cade became the rock star of the Grade 2s. The girls swooned over him because he acted like a little Romeo calling them 'beautiful' and 'cute'. The boys wanted to play along with him because he was the new kid who could draw SpongeBob characters like nobody's business and had all the girls talking. But most of all, the classmates were special. They understood Cade's challenges and wanted to show their support. They were encouraging, caring, sensitive and empathetic toward Cade. These kids were such a blessing. Likely, Mrs. Girardi's words had influenced the children's behavior, but I believe that these children came from a place of real love and excellent parenting. Cade was a lucky little man considering that the chance of it going the opposite way was equally possible.

I know that Mrs. Girardi had a special place in her heart for Cade. She gained satisfaction with every one of Cade's successes. He represented hope, I think, that others like him could flourish and be happy. I believe that's partly why so many people are drawn to him.

We were able to meet Cade's EAs, Mrs. Scianitti and Mrs. Sistilli, who were meeting with Nicole in the first week. Both ladies appeared to be about my mother's age. They are the most loving women I could ever meet. I had the joy of meeting the other EAs at Blessed Trinity as well, and my perception of them was quite similar. They are all mothers. I think that when a person chooses a career such as this, it obviously isn't to become a millionaire; it's much more rewarding and enriching than that. I'm convinced that this career attracts some of the most compassionate human beings. The school's EAs work with many different students with varying degrees of special needs.

Nicole offered advice and direction on how to address Cade's behaviors and described in detail his strengths and weaknesses. Mrs. Scianitti and Mrs. Sistilli were open to learning quick ABA strategies. The EAs grasped the ABA concepts very quickly and with strong understanding. James and I offered our full support to Mrs. Scianitti and Mrs. Sistilli to be firm with the ABA strategies and to never waiver from them. We explained that, like the therapists and us at home, they must not give Cade special treatment because of his diagnosis. As his parents, we gave them full reign to be the boss, and we expected Cade to follow their rules, not the other way around. Mrs. Scianitti and Mrs. Sistilli seemed really enthused by our suggestions. They gave their word that they would do their best with this new approach, and we made it clear to them that James and I were immediately accessible by phone to offer any advice or suggestions.

Nicole completed her one-week visit at Blessed Trinity to help with Cade's transition, and returned to her regular position at Shining Through without him.

By the second or third week, I began getting reports from Mrs. Sistilli or Mrs. Scianitti of tantrums occurring during class.

Apparently, Cade struggled with the transitions from subject to subject. Also, when a new topic was introduced, it would cause him terrible anxiety. Cade wanted to stay on topics of learning that he already mastered, and he would shut down when he would be forced to move on to something else. Processing new information was difficult for him, so Cade often retaliated with an outburst that lasted for an hour. He would collapse to the floor, kicking desks and chairs in his way. The EA on duty dealt with the problem perfectly. They would take him out into the hall until he settled down. Their stories would be told similarly on any given day. The ladies would tell him that his behavior was unacceptable so he would have to go into timeout or the "thinking corner" as we used to refer to it. Cade hated that. He responded very well to this because he knew that the "thinking corner" meant we were very disappointed with his conduct. Since Cade felt everyone's emotions, he also felt our disappointment. It was a really effective form of punishment for a while because he hated being removed from the rest of his friends and classmates, and the threat of that happening curbed his behaviors greatly. No number of tantrums or bad attitudes would prevent the work from getting done. Mrs. Scianitti and Mrs. Sistilli allowed Cade to have short breaks throughout the class period. They would negotiate like an ABA therapist, "First finish this page, and then you can work on your drawing for five minutes..." This method worked very well. When Cade realized that he would not be able to get away with opting out of new subjects and things that were unpleasant just because it made him angry, the exhausting challenge of learning and absorbing new material became tolerable to him over time. He required fewer and fewer breaks as time went on.

By the end of the school year, Cade's EAs had learned a great deal about how to get the most out of him academically. James and I hoped that Cade would be lucky enough to be placed with Mrs. Scianitti and Mrs. Sistilli again for Grade 3 because we trusted them, and they were truly on board with our tough love philosophy and approach.

Cade now had the joy of experiencing a whole summer off. He had some new friends over for play-dates, particularly a little girl named Alyssa who lived just a few houses away. She was his classmate and they'd hit it off immediately, like two peas in a pod. They established a bond of friendship that I never expected for Cade. Alyssa seemed to understand Cade fully. She had no negative judgement toward him, or any judgement for that matter. They just loved each other simply and innocently. Alyssa was mature in mind for her age, like a wise older woman, yet, pure and sweet. She would interact with Cade as if she was his older sister. It was a dream come true to see Cade being embraced and sought out by other children for the first time in his life.

Life had really changed for our family. Cade was flourishing so much that even he was aware of his improvements. Up until this time, Cade was the boy who asked for nothing, and for the first time in his life, he had a request that he had repeated over several weeks that we could not ignore: Cade wanted a backyard party to celebrate his achievements. James and I agreed that nothing would be more important or more fitting to celebrate. The fact that Cade wanted this for himself emphasized how much he had evolved. We felt strongly that this would not only be a party for Cade, but a party for Nève as well. She was an incredibly influential factor to Cade's rehabilitation that she deserved to be honored too.

On a Saturday near the end of August, we had about fifty friends and family in our backyard. Our guests included aunts, uncles, cousins, grandparents, some classmates, and old friends. Sarah and Amanda were also there. Kids were playing, music was blaring, James was at the barbeque, and the adults enjoyed each other's company and conversation while having a drink in the shade of our giant chestnut tree.

Cade wanted to make a speech. We weren't sure what he was

going to say, but we were eager to accommodate him. James had set up the karaoke machine outside earlier in the day for this occasion. When everyone had had their fill of burgers, treats and drinks, and James and I'd had some down-time, James invited Cade over to the microphone after he had thanked everyone for coming and explained the purpose of this celebration. Cade now loved attention and loved to stand before crowds. He didn't have a shy bone in his body. He hesitated for a second as he gathered in his mind the words and thoughts he wanted to relay. He thanked everyone for coming, and made some funny introductions, "I am Cade, and this is my mom, Tania. This is my dad, James. This is my sister, Nève..." this went on and on and everyone thought it was adorable. Cade, then, encouraged the guests to enjoy the bouncy castle we had rented and offered everyone the opportunity to use the pool.

James interrupted Cade with, "Tell them what we are celebrating, Cade."

The best part of Cade's announcement was his final statement, "I am Cade. I can talk now. I am no more autism." Well, it wasn't perfect grammatically, but no one gave a crap about that. He got the most resounding applause and support from everyone, and he rendered many to tears. James presented Cade and Nève with a plastic medal of achievement each from the dollar store which he placed around their necks. Afterward, Cade and Nève indulged in some singing and dancing with their cousins and friends at the microphone. It was a really fun afternoon that most of us will never forget.

When Grade 3 started in September, we arranged for Alyssa to be in the same classroom as Cade. Their friendship had built up over the summer and I thought it would be wonderful for Cade to experience Alyssa's positive influence in the classroom. We were so happy to learn that Mrs. Sistilli and Mrs. Scianitti were going to be Cade's EAs again as well.

This was going to be an exceptionally interesting school year because Nève was starting Grade 1 at Blessed Trinity. She was very excited to be going to the same school as her big brother. Nève was quick to make new friends, and she couldn't wait.

The first day back was a bit crazy. The class lists were posted on boards on the walls, and students were expected to find their name and then go line up with their classmates. Parents were allowed to enter school grounds to assist their children for the first week only. By the second week, parents were no longer permitted, so I had to make sure both children understood where they were meant to go. I had no trouble trusting Nève to follow my directions; it was Cade I was worried about. I wasn't confident that Cade had the under-standing to follow the instructions. I worried that he would get distracted by something – anything – and wander off, away from school property. Though the yard was well-staffed it didn't stop me from imagining the worst. I had some peace of mind from his sweet little classmates who would come up to us almost every morning with a friendly salutation and hugs. Often, a trio of girls that included Alyssa would come over to Cade and offer to hold his hand and get him to the line safely. They were an angelic group of kids.

Sometimes, however, there would be no classmates around. I would then ask Nève to walk her brother to his line and to keep an eye on him in case he wandered off. She was so burdened by my simple request. She was already like a three-foot teenager rolling her eyes and fussing from embarrassment. I would keep my eyes peeled to the best of my ability and pray.

On a couple of mornings when Cade's classmates were not around to take him to his line, I would notice Cade walking off in the distance heading away from the school. I had to catch the attention of a school attendant to let her know where he was. She chased after Cade in a panic. The other time this happened, I ignored the school rules and ran across the playground onto the public field to retrieve him. I wasn't going to take any more chances.

Eventually it was decided that Cade's EAs would meet him in the yard, as they had done during last school year, to ensure that he followed the morning protocol. By Grade 4, the wandering had stopped, and Cade had no difficulty lining up by himself.

Even though Cade was rapidly improving overall, there were the occasional days that he was quite defiant and very resistant. The EAs discovered that if they told Cade that his behavior would be reported to us and then we would put him on the "thinking chair" when he got home, he would almost always adjust his behavior. Cade was very affected by being placed on the "thinking chair." He would sit perfectly still while fighting back tears. When his time was up, he would almost always lash out at us as if we had offended him deeply. That response always resulted in Cade returning to the "thinking chair" until he was prepared to apologize and calm down. We would remind Cade of the reasons for his punishment to begin with. This would sometimes take a few cycles before Cade understood that we would not bend on the matter. As a parent, one of the keys to success when raising an autistic child is to never show powerlessness and never let them get away with negative behavior.

As Cade continued to progress, James and I began to incorporate the confiscation of Cade's Nintendo DSi into his punishments for bad behavior at school and at home. He adored that gadget and would spend hours making incredible moving cartoons on a program called Flip Notes. Mrs. Sistilli and Mrs. Scianitti would use this threat to control his behaviors in class, "I'll write a note to your mom and dad about your behavior and they will take your DSi away." It was perfect. This punishment helped Cade get into the pattern of good habits and behaviors at school, and there have been no more notes or news of bad episodes since.

Parents, temporarily, must play major roles along with the teachers and EAs in ensuring that their child understands how to act and behave while in school. We firmly instructed Cade's educators, right from the beginning, that his disability would never – and should never – be an excuse to be disruptive in the classroom or hinder his education. We urged a firm approach to teaching and assisting – it would be Cade's only hope for success. The teachers and assistants were thrilled to know that James and I were strong allies with them, and that we shared the common goal of giving Cade the most fulfilling academic experience possible, as well as a smooth and positive experience for them as his educators. We made it very clear that we were only a phone call away, and that nothing was impossible or too difficult to tackle.

The lines of communication need to be wide open between yourself and your child's educators, more so than with a typical kid. Eventually, this will no longer be as necessary as your child matures and gets a strong sense of what we, as parents, expect from them on a daily basis.

CHAPTER 14

OUR NORMAL LIFE

I'm at a loss for words at this point. I feel like the story ends here. Or perhaps this is where the story really begins.

Cade has had a very successful and happy few years since attending Blessed Trinity. His status as an artist has traveled throughout the school. His cartoony, wide-eyed character-drawings are playful and full of detail. In 2014, our family published a children's book that Cade illustrated. This book is filled with colorful and vibrant drawings conceived entirely by Cade, which includes a main character that Cade calls "Sabrina." The book is called *"How to Love Myself and Others."* Fittingly, it teaches children the importance of finding self-love, no matter what, and ways they could foster those feelings. James has been to several schools in Ontario and in the U.S. to read it and share its important message.

Cade just had his twelfth birthday, and Nève will be ten in May (2015). I feel like an ordinary mom with few tribulations, other than the regular ones that every parent faces. Our household feels more than normal, it feels pleasant.

Every day I drop the kids off at school. Cade and Nève leave the car together after arguing for most of the journey, and then they walk to their designated line-ups. I hate it when they argue, and I also love it when they argue – because it's *normal*. They are constantly bickering. Nève is the dominant sibling, but she gets her share of

Cade's retaliation. I like that she teaches Cade to be tough when he needs to be. She calls him names and provokes him, and he reciprocates. He was forced to learn to keep up and play the game or get clobbered. It's amazing to me that two kids with such polar differences can find enough common ground to fight over. Nève regularly teases Cade for the way he speaks, but I know it doesn't hurt him. Actually, I think it helps him. Of course, I wish the delivery of her corrections were kinder, but maybe they wouldn't be impactful enough for Cade otherwise. James and I get upset with Nève for her lack of compassion towards Cade, but maybe that's a good thing. She is the one person on this planet who truly treats her brother like he's not autistic. She doesn't bend and shape to suit his needs. Nève doesn't tolerate, from Cade, anything more than what she would tolerate from any of her male classmates – who are all gross and have cooties. She treats Cade like any little sister would treat her annoying older brother. Instead of lamenting this, James and I should probably be celebrating it. Maybe she's the fire that keeps Cade on his toes. When push comes to shove, however, Nève looks out for her big brother and makes sure he does the right thing. Cade only wishes his little sister would give him more hugs. Occasionally, I catch them playing beautifully together and it just warms my heart.

I go to work every day. I enjoy the adult interactions and working alongside James, my brother and my dad, at a desk at our distribution warehouse. It's not a glamorous job like the lifelong dream I had of becoming a singer/actor, but I get the flexibility I otherwise would not have at any other job.

When I pick up the kids from school, I can rely on seeing them walking toward the car. They have gained more independence since the days when I used to wait just outside the exit doors in the freezing weather. I gave the kids specific instructions on what to do during dismissal. Cade would have to wait for Nève to meet him at his classroom and they would then walk together to the car. There have been a handful of instances where one kid was absent from school and the other had to leave alone. But luckily Cade has become totally accustomed to changes, new ones and old ones, which is atypical for autistic people. He can adjust easily and naturally to anything that gets thrown his way. Cade has become so sure of himself, that even if Nève unexpectedly didn't turn up, he would figure out what to do without having a meltdown. This is a major turn of events, considering there was a time, not long ago, when Cade would have a violent tantrum if I was out of his sight for just a second in public.

We can now go anywhere and do anything as a family without having to worry about tantrums or obtrusive and imposing mannerisms affecting the flow of the day. For example, we don't have to plan an outing or an event around what may set off Cade, because nothing sets him off anymore. We addressed all quirks, demands, and idiosyncrasies when he was younger through ABA techniques and desensitization. Cade can be asked to do anything at any time, within reason, without any difficulty. He can now sit through church silently (but impatiently because he's still a kid, not a robot). There was a time when the sound of a filled church or auditorium would send him into fits of violent agony. James and I didn't understand this at first – Cade exhibited this behavior long before his diagnosis, when he was an infant, in fact. With some reflection and discussion, we realized that all the sound, visual stimulation, and energy exuded from other individuals was torture for a sensitive autistic child like Cade. Large places with many people can be unpleasant for some, but it was debilitating to him. During his baptism he screamed the entire time – my dad had to take him outside because he was being so disruptive.

That occasion reminds me of the many times when Cade was screaming, and we had to pack up and leave a restaurant because Cade was being too disruptive. On reflection, we've realized that these tantrums were motivated by his extreme sensitivity to noise and energy bouncing around. Perhaps the meltdowns in public bathrooms and malls were caused by the high acoustic echoes and sounds as well. James and I didn't understand that Cade was experiencing pain of some sort. It was a sensory matter that was too overbearing for a child to understand or process. Shortly thereafter, James and I figured out the reasons for Cade's outbursts in those situations. James admitted that, he too, has some aversions to these types of environments and large group settings. From there on, we approached similar situations with great consideration to Cade's sensitivities. The tricky part was not allowing his sensitivities to get in the way of having a normal life.

We had been to several children's concerts where the stadiums were filled with thousands of screaming kids, loud music, and flashing lights. We recognized that all the energy and stimulation was going to be an enormous challenge for Cade. So, when Cade and Nève were small, we made a point to go to as many concerts and performances as possible as a means to desensitize Cade, as well as fun for us all. I remember the first time we saw one of the Sesame Street Live shows that featured Elmo. On the way to the concert arena, James and I warned the kids (mainly Cade) that many, many people would be there. We explained with great enthusiasm how wonderful it will be to see all our favorite Sesame Street characters and hear all the songs being performed by them. As we entered the arena, James and I could tell it was a lot for Cade to take in. The energy of thousands of adults and children and all the bright lights set his senses into overdrive. We sat in our seats while Cade kept his face buried in James' chest. James had his hands over Cade's ears to try and make the experience more bearable. He talked and sang quietly to Cade to comfort him. We knew being there was going to be painful to Cade, so we took it slowly.

Nève, like all the other kids, was sitting up in her seat, enjoying the view and asking for treats and toys while anxiously waiting for the show to begin.

Finally, the music began. It was very loud. James subtly began to inch his hands away from Cade's ears as the introduction was well underway, while maintaining a firm hold of Cade's head. We gently encouraged Cade to turn his head as all the performers came onto the stage. "Oh look, Cade! I see Big Bird and Ernie! Oh, hi, Grover! Hi, Cookie Monster!" It was all too exciting not to, at least, take a peak.

As Cade apprehensively turned his head, we began to highlight all the details of the show with an uplifting tone. "Wow, look, it's Elmo! He is being so silly with his friends, and... hey... we know this song!" James and I talked softly into Cade's ear. Before you knew it, Cade was seated forward on James' lap and James had removed his hands completely from Cade's head. Cade was enjoying the show and was tolerating – and maybe joyfully accepting – the sensory overload. By the end of the show, Cade was standing on James' lap totally captivated by the sights and sounds of the performance.

Today, loud crowded places are no longer a challenge. In reality, the struggles relating to that are a distant memory.

Our lives have changed in insurmountable ways. Cade and Nève have a number of good and loyal friends from school with whom they have occasional play-dates. Cade and Nève have become expert swimmers since we installed a pool in our backyard. Swimming lessons was fine, but the weekly half-hour sessions didn't really give them the chance to truly feel confident in the water. The freedom to play in the water throughout the summers propelled them to advanced levels. Cade is a regular fish. He could stay underwater for reasonably lengthy periods of time and swim for most of the day. Nève is a more technically advanced swimmer than Cade, and though she enjoys swimming and playing in the water with friends, I don't think she loves it nearly as much.

From the time Cade was eight years old and Nève six, the kids have been going to summer camp every year for most of the season. A yellow school bus would pick them up in the morning and return them in the early evening. The camp is situated about forty minutes north from us where the area is very rural and woodsy. They learn skills such as archery, bouldering, rock climbing, crafts, and canoeing, to name a few. Nowadays, programs geared for children are equipped with the staff and tools to facilitate the differing needs of every child. People are more aware and open to integrating children with special needs into typical programs and this is remarkably heartwarming and progressive. I don't remember this many programs for special needs children when I was a child. I believe it was much more segregated. Sadly, in my opinion, no one truly benefitted from that thinking. The special needs children never had the chance to learn from their typically-developed peers and vice versa. Ironically, the typical children would likely gain much more from the child with special needs.

Cade and Nève have been going to Kettleby Valley Camp for the past four summers and it offers a camp-buddy system for campers with special needs for only an additional $50 per week. The previous camp they attended for two weeks during the Shining Through days, unfairly charged a whopping $375 extra per week and that made camp terribly hard to afford. The buddy was usually a fifteen or sixteen-year-old counselor-in-training. Cade had a buddy at camp and every summer we would get a more positive report on his attitudes and behaviors. Every day his camp-buddy would write a short note to let us know how Cade was getting on. James and I were able to respond to these notes. On a couple of occasions in the earlier years, we'd get reports of bad behavior but nothing too serious. We would reply, "Be the boss. He must never get away with inappropriate behavior. Please treat him and his behaviors as you would with any other camper. If you do time-out, we support that. If that fails, explain to him that you will write about it to his mom and dad." **That** worked every time. The worst punishment for Cade, to this day, is having his iPad or computer confiscated and he knew that would happen if we found out about his bad behavior.

This past summer, Cade didn't require a buddy at all, as he has grown mentally by leaps and bounds. He has gained so much independence this past year, and he no longer wanders or gets side tracked from group activities. Cade has developed so much body and spatial awareness, that he understands about danger and staying away from it which is why the wandering has stopped.

Summertime is still the most exciting and fun-filled time of year for us, and it is only getting better. As you know, going to Canada's Wonderland is one of the most regular things we do for the half a year it is open. Cade hasn't been given any line privileges since the days when we went with Sarah. He can wait patiently for very long periods of time in line without as much as a single complaint. Surprisingly on many instances, we have been waiting in an extra-long line for the front seat of a spectacular roller coaster ride, and just as our turn would come, we would have an individual with special needs take our turn – choosing the front seat, of course – and leaving us to wait one more turn. In the past, Cade would have had a meltdown over this – not because someone else took his turn, but because it broke the flow of his expectations. But now Cade is flexible. He needs an explanation like Nève, but nothing more. Often, many of the individuals with special needs happen to be autistic teenagers or adults. I quietly celebrate with the kids every time. "We don't need to do that anymore, Cade, because you have changed, and your behavior is better now." After some mild whining from Nève I would continue, "We should be thankful to God that you have come so far and be proud of the hard work you have endured to be so well today." I would further explain that the individual had difficulty waiting in long lines just like Cade had in the past. I would tell them that WE were the fortunate ones. Predictably, Nève would complain some more. At this point in her young childhood, she really needs to learn to exercise her compassion for autistic people because in her childish view, they all just get what they want. With Cade, all she remembers is the few privileges he receives due to his disability, not the endless barrage of struggles he confronts daily. Nève would always ask, "Can't we just get a special needs pass?"

My answer was always no.

We do not accept any more special permits. When our handicap parking permit expired, we knew that would be the beginning of a new era. It was more than a piece of paper - it was a symbol, an energy no longer attached to us. When it was tossed into the trash, we removed one less crutch from our lives and that empowered us as a family. Do I miss having a parking spot everywhere I go with Cade? A little, but I know what we have in exchange is a much greater gift.

We have been blessed with the means to travel to Disney World and Disneyland. We have had many road trips and adventures as a family. We have flown to Las Vegas to see James' parents, and this past Christmas was spent in Punta Cana in the Dominican Republic, with my parents and brother. Cade was a saint. He displayed no evidence of having autism. On one of these flights, we heard a screaming child at the front of the plane. He was not a baby, but about Nève's age. This boy screamed and kicked nearly for the entire flight. When I approached the front to use the lavatory, I recognized immediately what was going on. The little boy was frantically waving his hand by his head and kicking the wall in front of him as his parents desperately tried to console him in vain. I was almost moved to tears as I knew exactly how they were feeling – helpless. I wanted so much to give them advice and help them through this, but I was afraid my actions would further complicate the situation in their minds. But I simply could not stay quiet, "My little boy is like your little boy. Mine is twelve now and he's ok. It will get easier..." I smiled without judgment in the hope that they would feel my vibes of compassion. I hoped my words would be as true for them as it was for us. I hoped I wasn't misleading them, but I just had to give them some words of encouragement in their time of desperation. As the boy's anger continued unrelentingly I fantasized about getting on my knees in the aisle of that plane and breaking out in songs and dancing animatedly. What prevented me from doing so was the idea that it might not work! What worked for Cade was not the answer for everyone after all. I wasn't willing to find out because I chickened out. I don't know this child. I didn't want to upset the parents further. The father of the little boy had him on his lap as the boy was flailing his wrists trying to hit himself and his dad. All I felt that I could do was let them know that they were not alone and that they were understood.

I tried to send vibes of love to the boy. I knew he would have the ability to feel them, but the pain-energy from his parents surrounded him, and he was too deep into his own rage.

The most unique and evolved attribute that mainly autistic people behold is physical sensitivity, as I've already said. I enjoy tickling Cade from a distance. I look at him with intense concentration and love, and as he looks at me, I do the tickling motions with my fingers without even being within ten feet of him. He goes into fits of laughter and I tickle him right to the floor. Also, my voice alone can be felt by Cade. Again, with concentration and that deep feeling of love you get when you're elated, I make a high-pitched sound with my voice – it's the sound of love because that's what I decided it was – Cade feels it and responds to it warmly like I'm showering him with goodness. I know this because he returns it to me. So much can be taught to a person like this when the channels are open and free of negativity. If the vibration of love is felt everywhere in the child's environment, they will come out from their cocoon and succeed.

At school, Cade has had the opportunity to go on some field trips especially organized for the students with special needs, but we respectfully declined them all. We told the teachers, more than once, that we want to encourage Cade to be as much like his other peers as possible, and the fewer privileges he gets, the better off he will be. In Grade 3, Cade was nominated for an award for his artistic talents. We were thrilled when we heard that his teacher had nominated him for this award, but later, we discovered that it was for students with special needs. It was too late for us to back out, but had I known this ahead of time, James and I would not have accepted. Cade could have been nominated in any arts award program and done well. Honestly, we'd rather not put any labels on Cade at all that could possibly make him feel like he is not as capable as the mainstream of society. As his parents, I think it empowers him that he knows we view him as a regular kid. Set ambitious expectations for your child, no matter what the disability, and you may likely get the results. What you expect from your child is what you shall receive.

I had the opportunity to meet with Dr. Fabian about seven years since the last time he saw Cade. I asked him to re-assess Cade because we needed to update his papers, and because I wanted an excuse to come over and show him off. Cade was required to stay and perform tests with Dr. Fabian that would take about two hours per day for two days. I sat quietly outside the room while Cade was being tested. I heard a lot of the conversation and I was amazed that Cade replied so well to his questions, which was a staunch difference from years prior. I was so proud of Cade's performance. He did not whine or fuss, even though there were times he was getting bored by a certain test and would ask the doctor if this would take much longer. If Cade did not know the answer or was beginning to get frustrated with the type of question, and there were some, he would say "pass." Overall, I was impressed with Cade's patience. There were a few moments where I had been blown away by Cade's response to a question because I would not have been able to answer it any better myself.

After the test scores had been tallied and analyzed a few weeks later, Dr. Fabian had James and I come to his office to discuss the findings of the results. The results of the tests did not show me anything I didn't already know about Cade's weaknesses; it was determined that Cade had trouble processing heard and read information... not a surprise. What was exciting to James and I was that Cade had made major gains in all other fields, in which he scored average along with other children his age. When it came to thinking outside the box and problem solving, Cade scored well above average. Dr. Fabian concluded our discussion with a very positive remark, he said, "Continue what you are doing at home."

He explained that Cade had made such astounding growths that if we continued the way we had been going, he would surely have a bright and independent future. He told us that any new diagnosis of autism or Asperger's Syndrome now all came under the same term – Autism Spectrum Disorder (ASD), with no differentiation between higher or lower functioning, however, it was his opinion that Cade had Asperger's Syndrome, which is a high functioning autism, where individuals are capable of average, and in some unique cases, above average intelligence. This was a vast difference from where we had begun. At the age of two, Cade was deemed low functioning and would likely not be able to communicate. Today, we simply cannot shut him up!

Dr. Fabian informed us that only ten percent of autistic children made this sort of vast growth and change. James and I beamed with pride when we heard this statistic. Before leaving the office, Dr. Fabian gave us some straightforward tips on how to help Cade exercise the audio processing mechanisms. Though we still have some work ahead of us, I realize that Cade has the potential to nip this challenge – and any other – in the bud. I recall that earlier in his life, we thought Cade was totally deaf. Now, we can call him from a distant room on a different floor, and he will reply with no hesitation. This was a skill that was taught and was in no way a natural behavior for Cade. But, you would never know that seeing him today. Everything he does seems so organic. It was like everything we did earlier in his life like teaching him to eat solid food, look into our eyes when communicating, and teaching him to respond to his name, had rewired his brain somehow. Nothing is impossible or too difficult to teach Cade. He rides a two-wheel bike effortlessly, and he has a passion and talent to create and post his own YouTube videos. Cade shares his love of Minecraft, a computer game that fosters creativity, with countless others including many of his classmates. At one time he avoided other children but now he has friends to play with.

Cade is growing academically. He is not at the level of his peers because his curriculum is about a year and a half behind on average, but Cade continues to make gains and the level of difficulty of his work increases every term. The point is that Cade is happy, flourishing, and beaming with potential for new growth and development. He has proven this to us time and time again.

Here is the secret to success going forward with your gorgeous gifted child:

- *Stop using the word autistic to describe your child or when referring to your child.* Use it only when necessary, otherwise don't! Society has attached negativity to that word and that's why it is poisonous. Keep that energy away from your family and definitely from your child. For example, we tell curious people that Cade has a little trouble processing what is said, so it is necessary to talk clearly, but even that is rare now. People are so aware and accepting of the differences in others that, more often than not, I never have to explain.

- *Never allow autism to be an excuse for negative, weird or odd behavior.* If your child was typical, ask yourself, "Would I allow him/her to do this?" This is the general ABA platform. Do not permit your child to engage in hand flapping, rocking or whatever, in public. Let your child let off steam in the privacy of their own bedroom or their own space instead.

- *Never EVER compare your child to others!* Your child is perfect in His own image. The sooner you learn that, the sooner you will bring peace into the family which is the *foundation* for real healing and growth.

- *Champion every tiny success your child makes.* Let him/her know how proud you are of their successes! Reward all positive behaviors.

- ***This is the hard one: SURRENDER!*** Autistic kids are highly, highly sensitive! They feel your pain whether you, in fact, are aware of it or not. If you carry pain over your child's diagnosis, you are only hindering their ability to develop and heal... I promise. Also, if your marriage or other close relationships are struggling, fix them first. Your child will not be as likely to advance if pain brought on from strained relationships is present. When I surrendered, Cade had the biggest developmental growth ever! Happy moms have happy children.

God chose us to raise these incredible treasures, our awesome children. There's a wonderful message He's trying to give us. It's up to us to understand it and learn it.

I have become so appreciative, not just for Cade's progress alone, but with everything. Like never before, I can truly appreciate all the gifts that have been blessed upon me. My health is getting significantly better because I fuel my body with positive thoughts – some negative – but mostly positive. Negative thoughts don't run my life anymore. I have control of them. When I feel negative, I recognize the emotion and try to correct it with some deep breaths and changing my thought process. Sometimes, even that is difficult. So, there are days I feel down in the dumps, I know the negative entity is there. Being aware of the negativity is a major part of eliminating it. On very rare occasions, I just surrender to the negativity knowing that it will pass, as I will never allow it to burrow a hole into my soul to establish permanent residence again. I let it linger for a day if it wants, but I know that in most cases, a good night's sleep is all I need to show it the exit. It comes as quickly as it goes. I discuss my feelings with James and he helps me to rationalize and find focus. We keep each other grounded. Our marriage is better than ever as James and I are growing as individuals and following our own passions and life journeys and supporting each other every step of the way.

I'm doing amazingly well. I've found real peace in my life. I don't suffer anymore because of autism. Autism is omitted from my daily conversations and it rarely – if ever – makes its presence into my thoughts. Our family and I see Cade for what he is capable of, what he has accomplished, what he has overcome, and the incredible miracle he will continue to be. No one ever worries or focuses on what he can't do, what he hasn't yet done, or what he will never be able to do, because that is only poison to the family, especially Cade himself. We understand that every person on Earth has some sort of challenges they will face – that's life. Everyone will confront adversity at some point in their lifetime – but it's how you address that adversity that counts. I believe I overcame my real greatest hardship in life and I'm confident that I will be able to confront more in the future as a stronger person. I have learned so much from my experiences as Cade's mom and I wouldn't trade those lessons for the world. Again, I have become grateful – a virtue I lacked before my role as a mother. I have become peaceful and totally fulfilled with my life. The negativity that society associates with autism is no longer attached to me or my family because I understand fully now that there is no poison more dangerous to Cade and our family. My happiness is Cade's medicine. He has proved this to the world.

I wish a similar – and better – outcome for every mother, father, and loved one who has been informed that their child or children have autism. It is not a curse. It is not a punishment. It's a different challenge to the one you were expecting. Raising any child is not easy because every person on Earth faces hardship in one way or another, whether it may be medically, emotionally, or circum-stantially related. Obstacles and challenges come with every child, but how a parent chooses to face these challenges makes all the difference in the world for that child's outcome.

I wish you happiness, peace, love, joy, fulfillment, good mental and physical health, empowerment, and the ability to surrender.

The End

UPDATE

As I'm writing this, it's April 2018! This book-publishing endeavor has been a painfully slow process with all the procrastinating and "life" getting in the way. I feel like before my final push to publishing, I need to add this conclusion since SO MUCH has happened since I wrote my farewell notations ending Chapter 14.

Cade has started high school last September, and this past January, he turned fifteen. He is transforming into an amazing, young man. He towers over me - not that that's hard to do – and all the normal things that come along with puberty are in motion. Like his peers, his desire to fit in is strong. In a crowd, he looks no different from anyone else. He acts like a very average student as he exhibits no stims or quirks. He has a ton of very friendly school mates who have known him since elementary school, and many who he just met during his brief time in ninth-grade. Cade is well protected by those many kids from the neighborhood and his former school who love him, from the rough students who tend to start trouble. He doesn't have any close friends, or a best friend, but he seems happy. He doesn't get invited out by anyone, but I don't think he's too bothered by it.

Academically, Cade is involved in some classes that are specific to students with learning challenges. Science, math, English, etc..., are all taught in small-group settings where the teacher has a more personal approach with each student. He also has classes like phys-ed., digital media, and Learning Strategies that include all students. In the first semester, Cade had science class with five other students. He had the learning experience of his life, and loved it! Like never before, he had the opportunity to do fun, hands-on science projects in class along with his teacher and peers, such as creating mini robots and electrical circuits. He planted seeds in a pot and got to bring home a parsley plant at the end of the course. Cade enjoyed the hands-on learning approach to this class, as he is mainly a visual learner. He finished that class with his highest grade, a 76%. Cade learned the periodic table by memory, and because he loved it so much, Ms. Watt, his teacher, allowed him to make a word-search for the other classmates, which incorporated only the periodic symbols. I know that you must be realizing the neat co-incidence of Cade's science teacher's name, right?

Cade received three-and-a-half credits out of a possible 4 for the first semester, more than we anticipated. One of his selected courses was only valued at half a credit. This means, Cade passed every class.

Our expectations of Cade are ambitious but entirely realistic. As I mentioned earlier in the book, as parents, we need to place our focus on our children's strengths and guide them into fields that embrace their strengths. Cade struggles a lot with academics due to his processing abilities, so we outlined a plan with the head of the special-needs department that will allow him to participate in courses that will serve him in the future. An issue came up earlier in the year where the school heads were suggesting that Cade would likely require two or three extra years of schooling to receive a high-school diploma. James and I were not agreeable with this forecast because we understand how it would be harmful to Cade to watch his peers graduate and move on long before him. That would tear apart his confidence and self-esteem, which is a huge propelling factor in his general growth. Our hope for Cade is that he will finish high-school successfully. What does that mean to James and me? We don't expect an 80% average - we root for passing versus failing. So far, so good. Cade will not be going to college or university after high-school, so our end goal doesn't have to look the same as it would for most of the other students. This philosophy of mine does not just apply to Cade; it will apply to Nève too. College and/or university will be an option to her if she wants it and if she needs it. Otherwise, James and I will not force post-secondary education upon her. Through the people we know and our own personal experiences, post-secondary education is not the "make it" or "break it" reason to one's success in life, and nor will it be for Cade. Ms. Arista, the head of the special-needs department at Cade's school, came up with an interesting solution to allowing Cade an opportunity to graduate with his peers. I did not know this before our meeting, but it turns out that a student can graduate from high-school with a "certificate" instead of a diploma. In Ontario, this means that a student may graduate earning a certificate with just fourteen credits (including seven compulsory) opposed to the thirty-two (including fifteen compulsory) for a diploma. James and I were completely on-board with this plan. With this new set goal, Ms. Arista and the school guidance team, will integrate more courses throughout the remainder of high-school that might interest Cade and supply him the tools to thrive in a workplace environment. Courses such as photography, broadcasting, drama, art, and digital media will nurture creativity, and they will help Cade explore these different forms of media. We were excited by the idea that Cade would have a fulfilling high-school experience that would consist of him exercising independence and acquiring knowledge he would likely use in his endeavors of working in the children's entertainment field.

It would be a travesty if I didn't share with you the lead-up to high-school. It was no walk in the park! I more than freaked out at the idea that Cade would be going to high-school. I imagine that it's terrifying for most parents - now throw in some of the history we had with Cade - it was petrifying!

Cade was very sad to leave Blessed Trinity. He understood he had to move on, but he didn't like it. Many of his friends were going to his high-school, and many were not. We chose this particular school, St. Elizabeth C.H.S., after investigating three others, because it is an art school. St. Elizabeth offers comprehensive art programs that include visual arts, dance, drama, vocal and music, for which one must be accepted through an auditioning process to participate throughout the entirety of high-school. This is called the Regional Arts Program, more commonly known as RAP. This year, they introduced into the program a new art medium; digital arts. This is computerized visual art. This class teaches students about the computer programs that facilitate the creations of modern-day animations and other forms of media. This was a no-brainer for me and James. We signed up Cade for an audition and he got accepted.

I was really worried – as usual – that Cade would not be able to keep up in this digital-media class. He would not be allowed to have an assistant as this class was very exclusive to the strongest students. I learned that the pace of this class was very fast and I was concerned that Cade would be left in the dust. It was early on at the beginning of the year that my concerns were justified. Cade was struggling to follow the curriculum. No amount of talent on Cade's part would permit him the ability to keep up to the high, intense pace of the class. He will continue with the RAP program until the end of ninth-grade, but by next school year, Cade may take the non-RAP version of digital media, depending how the rest of the school year goes. It is a lot less demanding and probably more fun. The head of the digital media class assured us that he would support Cade in developing a portfolio throughout high school, so he would have something substantial and impressive when he graduates.

The transition to high-school was a hell of a lot easier than I thought it would be. I think the change in atmosphere, new students and high expectations of Cade really brought out the best in him. With some mild help from aides, he knew that he would be expected to be more independent, and have more responsibility. Cade's desire to appear more mature and to fit-in influences his behaviors. The other students have been quite supportive and friendly. Cade is well known and loved by those who grew-up with him, that there is always someone to protect him from students who know him less and may tease or put him down. Overall, he has no problems with bullying... thank God!

Due to Cade's remarkable swimming abilities and love of water, my dad felt compelled to enroll him into a swimming course which will eventually lead him into competitive racing. My dad jokes that Cade is built like a swimmer, just like Michael Phelps, and he'd love to see where he could take his athletic abilities. Now that Dad is retired, he has the time to spend supporting Cade in this new adventure. It turns out that Dad was right! Cade is fast! He looked a bit clumsy at first, but these classes have been tightening his technique and increasing his speed very quickly. This is super thrilling for the family. Cade doesn't like instruction of any kind, but when he realized he has a gift that singles him out in a positive way, he has been so much more accepting and receptive of the lessons. We are all cheerleading him along. Who knows where swimming will take him, if not only for the enrichment of his life.

This summer, Cade is planning to start training as a camp counsellor at Kettleby Valley Camp. Since he was a camper there for six years, the staff was willing to accept him into the Leader in Training program. This is another opportunity for Cade to build confidence and self-empowerment as he will begin a new chapter in his life as a role-model to younger campers. He is required to spend an entire week without us as he will be sleeping there and not returning home like he normally does. Cade expressed some worry about that (me too), but we told him that it's important to do these types of things to help him gain maturity. Cade embraces that. Besides, we are a phone-call away.

Cade is turning out to be an amazing adult. Today, I could not have anticipated a better situation since the day of his diagnosis. I will support, encourage and cheer him on with every little step he takes. I will do it with love, pride and great enthusiasm. I will never look back on our journey with any sense of regret or sadness, and I will continue to push forward optimistically. I feel joy like never before. I choose to vibrate positive energy into our family, since Cade – especially – grows off it. Today, I know Cade can do anything. Never, ever give up!

NOW, The End

To contact the author, please visit
www.livinglaf.com or email at info@livinglaf.com

CPSIA information can be obtained
at www.ICGtesting.com
Printed in the USA
LVHW021032131019
633991LV00008B/28/P